19868

Goodenough
The church in the Roman
Empire

The Berkshire Studies in European History

GENERAL EDITORS

RICHARD A. NEWHALL
LAURENCE B. PACKARD
SIDNEY R. PACKARD

THE CHURCH IN THE ROMAN EMPIRE

BY

ERWIN R. GOODENOUGH
YALE UNIVERSITY

COOPER SQUARE PUBLISHERS, INC.
NEW YORK
1970

PREFACE

The college teacher of general European history is always confronted with the task of finding adequate reading for his classes which is neither too specialized and technical nor too elementary. For many topics, including several of the greatest importance, no such material is at the moment available. Moreover, in too many instances, good reading which undeniably does exist is in the form of a chapter in a larger work and is therefore too expensive for adoption as required reading under normal conditions.

The Berkshire Studies in European History have been planned to meet this situation. The topics selected for treatment are those on which there is no easily accessible reading of appropriate length adequate for the needs of a course in general European history. The authors, all experienced teachers, are in nearly every instance actively engaged in the class room and intimately acquainted with its problems. They will avoid a merely elementary presentation of facts, giving instead an interpretive discussion suited to the more mature point of view of college students.

No pretense is made, of course, that these *Studies* are contributions to historical literature in the scholarly sense. Each author, nevertheless, is sufficiently a specialist in the period of which he writes to be familiar with the sources and to have used the latest scholarly contributions to his subject. In order that those who desire to read further on any topic may have some guid-

v

ance short bibliographies of works in western European languages are given, with particular attention to books of recent date.

Each *Study* is designed as a week's reading. The division into three approximately equal chapters, many of them self-contained and each suitable for one day's assignment, should make the series as a whole easily adaptable to the present needs of college classes. The editors have attempted at every point to maintain and emphasize this fundamental flexibility.

Maps and diagrams will occasionally be furnished with the text when specially needed but a good historical atlas, such as that of Shepherd, is presupposed throughout.

R. A. N.
L. B. P.
S. R. P.

CONTENTS

CONTENTS

FOREWORD

THE reader of this little summary may be interested to know in advance the point of view from which it is written. Critical historical scholarship investigates Christianity as it would Mithraism or Confucianism, with no preconceived value-judgments as to whether its origin was a blessing or an injury for the development of mankind; with no more or less prejudice for the veracity of Luke than of Plutarch; and with the hypothesis that probably Christianity was in at least one respect like all other religions, namely that it was a summation of various religious ideas of the environment inherited from the past, with some new added force to give it distinctness.

With this hypothesis in mind the historian investigates all other religions and philosophies that impinged upon the societies in which Christianity developed, in order to visualize with historical accuracy what new things Christianity added, and what was the source and significance of the ideas and practices which Christianity took over from others. Everyone will agree at least to the extent of seeing such a precursor of Christianity in Judaism; critical historians seek and admit evidence of similar relationships with other religions. This evidence is largely philological, and so would help the general reader very little if he had it. For we have

no great collections of letters, diaries, or public documents to give direct evidence for our statements. The
source material of the first century and a half of Christianity would not overflow two bulky volumes. What
the historian must do is to analyze every syllable of
this, reject what seems not reliable by the general
canons of historical criticism, and then, by investigat-
ing the significance of the terminology used, come to
a richer understanding of the documents than a simple
reading could give. Such analysis can never interest
anyone but the specialist. Of general methodology it
need only be said further that like every historian the
man who uses this sort of evidence does so on the
assumption that two developments of the same idea
are unlikely to have occurred in the same region simultaneously without relation to each other, or to a common original, and he applies this assumption to Christianity just as to any other religion. Of course the
assumption is not demonstrable, but it is used because
it is the most probable guess, as Plato would have
called it; and history is never anything more, especially in the ancient field.

But as we attempt thus to reconstruct the story on
the basis of historical data, and to avoid value-judgments while we keep as far as possible to matters of
attested fact, any man is free to go on and believe
much more about early Christianity than we feel we
can assert historically. As to the divinity of Jesus,
for example, we have as historians nothing to say one
way or the other. The fact that there is for it no historical evidence in the orthodox meaning of that term

by no means prevents one from believing that Jesus was the Second Person of the Trinity. That statement, which the Church has always taught as a matter of revelation, is quite as tenable when we admit how little historical record there is of Jesus as when we do not. This and other doctrines are matters of faith, for, by reserving the right to interpret Scripture for herself, the Church has long implied that she regards the written evidence as ambiguous or inadequate when approached by rational analysis alone.

The difference between the historian's and the churchman's points of view was beautifully illustrated by a story told by the late Dr. F. C. Conybeare of Oxford, one of the greatest critical historians in the field during his generation. He was at one time seated at dinner beside a learned Catholic priest, who suddenly turned to him and said, "Conybeare, of course you don't believe in the Virgin Birth?" Dr. Conybeare was surprised, but answered that to admit so amazing a contradiction of what we know of the laws of nature would need more evidence than we possess. "Quite right," said the priest, "you are not a Catholic; you have no right to believe in the Virgin Birth." What the priest meant was that he admitted that the evidence on its face value was insufficient; only the additional belief, that if the Church accepted it as genuine it must be true, could convince an intelligent man.

Traditional Protestantism, by regarding the Bible as a verbally correct revelation from God, likewise supplements and corrects the findings of human reason. It is without reference to any "additional source of truth

of divine origin" that the following story is told. No
one who understands the problems of evaluating scanty
evidence, and of writing brief summaries of large subjects, will think that it could be a complete statement
of the truth in any totally objective sense.

THE CHURCH IN THE
ROMAN EMPIRE

CHAPTER I

THE RISE OF THE CHRISTIAN CHURCH

It is generally understood that the great civilization of the Roman Empire was an extraordinary complex of ideas, institutions, and practices, borrowed from every part of the known world, but all joined into, and in part assimilated by, the Roman genius for organization. Ancient civilization had produced many remarkable systems of law, philosophy, religion, and commerce which the Romans came to dominate, and used rather than destroyed. Indeed some of these institutions the Romans so took to themselves and established that they survived even the crash of the Empire itself. So the Roman imperial law could never be forgotten, nor the religion to which the dying Empire turned for consolation. Of all that came out of the classical period to subsequent centuries nothing remotely compares with the Christian religion in its abiding influence upon the public and private life of men. If it is now difficult to get many modern types of people interested in that religion, or to guide them by its teaching, that should never blind the student of history to the fact that in by far the greater part of the past which he is hoping to understand Christianity has been accepted by every walk of men in Europe as the unquestioned arbiter of all existence. The following chapters try to tell the

3

story of how that religion began, what it claimed for itself, how it grew into the great organization of the Church, how it developed governmental claims and powers, as well as why it succeeded in winning the loyalty of the race.   For the Church is like some great personal genius in that it is easier to understand his greatness when we have heard the story of his early environment and youth.

No religion can have any general appeal which does not at least seem to offer to men what they feel they deeply need.   Christianity was and is no exception to the rule.   It succeeded at first fundamentally because it offered to the Græco-Roman world into which it came, and of which it was largely a product, the kind of comfort and inspiration which men were seeking.   When the Greeks were at the height of their powers they had taught that the universe is a great ordered system of which man is a part, and hence that the only right way to live is first to try to understand this ideal order of nature, and then to make one's life fit into it.   In public life that meant the most thoughtful coöperation in affairs of state; in private it meant the organization of body and mind in such a way that each part of one's being had its place, yet so that man's natural guide, his reason, kept all other parts from overstepping their proper bounds.   In the Hellenistic Age, that is, during the centuries between Alexander and the beginnings of Christianity, this ideal had been interpreted by leaders

of thought as a demand that man so rationalize his life
that he be completely independent of fortune, even in-
different as to the outcome of his endeavors, an ideal
which man hoped to achieve by simplifying his desires
so that he would expect to find happiness not in the
acquisition and enjoyment of external goods, but in the
ability to be content with what he happened to have.
The supreme virtue was thus the dominance of reason
in one's life, resulting in contentment with life as it
comes. Such at least was the ideal life as described by
philosophic writers of almost every Hellenistic school,
and with them, while frequently only a pose, it was for
many a passionate quest; and yet that it had much
appeal to ordinary men may seriously be doubted.

In any case by the beginning of the first century
before Christ a great mass of men were finding increasing help in the teaching of those who confessed the inability of man, as he naturally is, to keep his passions
and desires always subject to his reason, and who
sought to discover in some form of religion a door to
a larger life, in which his reasoning faculty, too weak
to control his life, might be enlarged and strengthened.
For the various philosophies which were monotheistic
had taught that the mind or reason of man was a bit of
God living in him. Why not then appeal to God to
give more of Himself, to make the reason fragment in
man larger and stronger? If such an addition to one's
natural powers could be achieved, that would be truly
salvation, as the age called it, by which was meant an
assurance of safety in the vicissitudes of this world, as
well as in that next world to which all men were look-

ing with restless expectation. It was thought that this divinity, which man hoped to find revealed in religion so that he could take it into himself, was not so much God himself as a radiation out from God. The ancient world was still full of sun-worship, or of figures and conceptions derived from sun-worship, so that God was thought of as the sun sending out to men God-rays, as the sun radiates sun rays. Now as the sun warms and brings life into the physical world, so, it was thought, these God-rays, coming into men's lives, warm and enliven their minds, making them grow and become strong, until men can meet the trials of life with happy security. This radiating aspect of deity was called by many names, Word, Spirit, Savior, Creator, Lord, Divine Law, Natural Law, Power of God, Reason, Wisdom, all of which suggest slightly different aspects of a conception which properly included them all and many more.

The expansion of one's own reason, or spirit, by the incoming of this Divine Spirit, then, to use the only term of the lot which has kept any of its original meaning, was regarded as the solution of life's problems. But how was it to be accomplished? Where could the Spirit be found? The majority of men thought like their primitive ancestors that they could secure and use spiritual power by means of magical charms, passwords, and incantations. Others had a higher and more mystical aspiration, to find it by direct action of God in their own hearts. But all regarded its coming as marking the victory of the higher spiritual part of man over the material and bodily, and as a sure guarantee of happy existence after death. And all people of the age, barring only a few of the most severe thinkers, hoped to find this Spirit not by unaided rational or mystical efforts, but with the help of some divinely revealed external rite or sacred book which would show timid and heart-hungry humanity the Way, the Road, to Life. That is, the Hellenistic Age witnessed one of the most momentous changes of history: men lost the reliance of thoughtful Greeks of the Classical Age upon the accumulation of truth by human reason and investigation, and turned instead to ask God to reveal the truth to them. The imparting of this revelation was regarded as a divine illumination, or, as they sometimes called it, a new spiritual birth, and it would come as the reward not of the exertion but of the prostration of human effort. If ever mankind could be convinced that such a revelation had been found, human effort and cares in this life must be completely and permanently subordinated to the higher world and its demands.

This great new emphasis upon the value of external revelation arose partly because of the breakdown of philosophic initiative and moral courage, but also because the Greek world discovered in the Orient and Egypt many religions, themselves age-old though new to the Greeks, which suggested the possibility of discovering such a revelation. In many oriental countries sacred rites of majestic dignity and mystery celebrated the deities who had for centuries, if not millenniums, been represented as meeting half-way the same feeling of human helplessness and guilt as that which the Hellenistic peoples were experiencing. Most of these religions had also a sacred book or literature which seemed to reveal unplumbed depths of wisdom when expounded by those who understood them. These books, it was thought, had been dictated by the Spirit to some holy man or men who had written them down without error, so that they were a valid guide to spiritual things, were, indeed, the truth direct from God.

The first important religion of this type in the Greek world was Orphism, which from the sixth century B.C. had been growing from a small beginning to great influence. It taught the uselessness of this life, man's sinfulness and need of redemption because of his inability to save himself without divine help; and it solved its own problem in an elaborate ritual in which the believer became "enthusiastic," that is, filled with the saving deity. Long before the beginning of the Christian Era the sacred stone and rites of the Great Mother, a religion of Asia Minor, had been taken to Rome, as well as the Sibylline Oracles, supposed utterances of inspired women. Two other religions, that of the saving Mithra from Persia, and of Isis, Mother of Heaven and the Gods, from Egypt, were making a deep mark upon the life of the entire civilized world, for the devotees of both insisted that in their rites, scriptures, and pass-words the desire of the Hellenistic Age for a saving revelation of deity had been met. The "saving deity" in all these religions was interpreted as a personalized symbol for the Spirit which men were seeking, so that union with the special "savior" in a rite meant union with God's beneficent Spirit.

Everywhere still another religion, Judaism, was ex-

citing interest, though the Jews were only just beginning to rise above their racial prejudices. Many Jews
still wanted to keep their religion to themselves, or to
require of all converts a strict observance of the Jewish
customs and taboos which would make them ridiculous
in the eyes of their Greek and Roman fellow citizens.
Yet other Jews, especially many who lived out in the
Græco-Roman world, themselves affected by the spirit
of the times, were not slow to see the advantage they
had in their Scripture, and to represent it to all men
as the ancient and only genuine revelation of God.
Since approximately 400 B.C. Judaism had become,
especially in Egypt under the Ptolemies, a missionary
religion, "compassing sea and land to make one convert," and apparently presenting itself in Greek terms,
like the other oriental religions, as the Way to the
Spirit.

Each of these religions, as well as many others, had
its special appeal. Orphism offered the Spirit through
ancient rites and enthusiasm. The beautiful Sun-God
Mithra had his atoning slaughter of a sacred bull, by
which his devotees might be benefited. In the ceremony of initiation into another mystery, that of Cybele,
a bull was butchered in such a way that its blood
streamed down over the initiate, making him a partaker
in the very life and spirit of the god himself. These
mysteries, then, released for men the purifying and
saving forces of the universe. Isis, the lovely distraught
mother, who found and collected the scattered pieces
of her beloved's slaughtered body, and brought him
back to life, represented the deeply desired compassion

and love of God for men, God's philanthropy, as they
called it, which would heal their broken lives and assure
them a happy life after death.   Demeter, seeking her
daughter Persephone, was the saving *mater dolorosa* of
antiquity.   And Jews, who had the most magnificent
body of revealed writing of any religion, had with it an
ability to dominate the material environment which excited the envy of those who ridiculed them for their
peculiarities.   Yet all these religions by their ritual and
moral discipline rather led the initiate up to deity than
brought the deity down to men.   Or perhaps the two
might be regarded as meeting half-way.   But the deity
did not come down and dwell with men in any permanently accessible form.   He or she remained remote,
approachable only by mystery and rite, and, as a result
of the expense of initiation, frequently accessible not
at all to the poor.   If, then, there should come a religion which would offer such Scriptures and moral
achievement as Judaism, such enthusiasm as Orphism,
such vividly enacted dispensation of spiritual rebirth
as Cybele and Eleusis, such passionate yearning love in
deity as Demeter and Isis, together with magnificent
ritual in which the lower classes might participate, it
would be a great religion indeed.   But if to these it
could add a concreteness of conviction, a belief that
deity, in his love of men, had actually come down in the
flesh and lived with men, loved the poor, helped the
suffering, and then had died an agonizing death for
mankind, but had conquered that death by coming
back to life afterwards; and that now, having gone
back to reign with God as before, he was acting as

mediator and helper for men; and that he had left behind on earth his Spirit in which men could be reborn
and live, die and rise again: could such a story be told
by men who could say "I saw him with my own eyes,
touched him with my own hands," then the religious
need of the age would be met. The story of early
Christianity is the story of the rise and conquest of a
religion which offered just this appeal.

JESUS

The early years of Christianity by no means suggested its tremendous future. At the beginning of the
Christian Era the Jews who lived in Palestine were one
of the few nations of the Roman Empire who were
rebellious against Roman domination, for their religious
beliefs were completely at variance with the presence
of Roman soldiers and rulers in the holy city of
Jerusalem. At least an active minority among them
believed that their God was to lead them to victory,
that the Jews were the chosen people of the world, and
the fact that they and their religion must be under the
control of heathen outsiders horrified them as the very
height of blasphemy against God. Their rage at such a
situation could find relief only in ardent hope that
some leader would come to cast off the Roman yoke,
and lead Israel not only to freedom but even to
domination of those who now were ruling over them.
Josephus, the Jewish historian, suggests that there was
a succession of individuals, each of whom thought that
he could play the part of this deliverer. Each stirred

up a mob of excited followers, and each in turn was overthrown, until finally Jerusalem and all Jewish national life perished with them.

— In the midst of this age of hatred for the Romans, there appeared a preacher in Palestine, about 28 A.D. He was a young carpenter from the north country of Galilee, of whose past we know nothing except that his home was in Nazareth, and that his family consisted of his mother Miriam, or Mary, her husband Joseph and several other children. His own name was Joshua, or in the Greek form, Jesus. Jesus too turned men's faces forward to a time of coming happiness for the Jews, which would be ushered in by the advent of the promised deliverer. At first Jesus apparently did not identify himself with this coming Messiah, as the deliverer was usually called by the Jews, though after he had been preaching for some time, he did so identify himself, at least to his chosen circle. His conception of the blessed future condition he was preaching is variously interpreted, but seems to have been two-fold: he believed that it was not yet here, and was going to be ushered in by a demonstration of power from God, when the heavens would be opened and God be fully revealed; yet he also taught that in a sense the "Kingdom of God," the usual term for this state of ideal social happiness, was already here in the hearts of men who were living true and upright lives. Consequently, while he turned men's faces toward the future, at the same time, like the great Jewish prophets of old, he turned their eyes inward, and showed them that true goodness was not a matter of what man did, so much as what he wanted to do. The only foundation for a right life, he taught, was an attitude toward all men of self-forgetting love. He insisted that man should live with man not in hatred and self-seeking, but in genuine loving kindness. He denounced the use of force between men to settle any dispute whatever. If people want ever to beat or rob you, he said, let them do with you as they please. Personal ambition, love of money, pride, narrow patriotism which expresses itself in hatred of one's national foes, indeed most of the qualities ordinarily respected by men, Jesus denounced, and told men to live improvidently like the birds and flowers, and unselfishly and lovingly together.

While Jesus thus denounced the qualities which most men admire, he turned upon all the respectable classes of the Jews. With the people of learning, the scholars, the professional religious classes, with rich men, he would have nothing whatever to do unless they met him upon his own ground. Since this rarely happened he sought companionship among the outcasts of society, for he found a congeniality with such people which he did not find with the respectable classes of Palestine. For followers he chose not young men from good families, but for the most part workers in the humblest occupations and trades in the social scale.

These people did not, of course, understand him fully. They talked together in perplexity about his strange doctrines, but they felt in him a personal power so great that, as though bewitched, they followed him wherever he went. Occasionally a man is born of such powerful personal magnetism that men seem to lose all sense of their own interests and ambitions in the longing to be with and to serve him, a phenomenon especially familiar in the ancient world.

How long Jesus preached we do not know, but probably not more than three years, perhaps only one. At one time he seemed to be very popular, so that the Jewish crowds, who were impressed by his character without understanding his ideas, wanted to compel him to become their general against the Romans. To escape such a contradiction of his hopes, Jesus retired to lonely or remote places for a time with his special followers, and only returned, finally, to attend at Jerusalem, with all good Jews, the great annual feast of the Passover.

Up to this time, Jesus had apparently avoided attracting attention to himself personally, in his endeavor to center men's attention upon his teachings. Now he strangely changed his methods, and deliberately provoked the crowd to hail him on his entry into Jerusalem as the long-expected king and deliverer of the Jewish people. He so well succeeded that his entry was a magnificent triumph, with shouting crowds following and acclaiming him the long-desired leader. But Jesus did not do as the crowd expected. His first move was popular with the crowd, but a challenge to mortal combat with the priestly factions. For instead of using his new authority to attack the Roman governors, as his followers had expected, Jesus turned against those who were profiteering in the Temple, that is, against the Jewish hierarchy itself. With kingly majesty (but without any record of violence)

Jesus ordered the people making money from the Jewish sacrificial rites to leave the Temple, and no greater tribute to his personal power could be paid than was done when these profiteers meekly obeyed his command. In the space they had occupied, Jesus now gathered his new following, to denounce the Jewish hierarchy and teach the strange principles of his kingdom.

The members of no upper class are tolerant when approached by a successful insurgent from the classes beneath them, who proposes to ruin their business, and who openly proclaims what seem to them to be libelous absurdities about their characters. Only one answer could have been expected from human nature under such circumstances: Jesus had attacked the Jewish aristocracy in both these ways, and so he must be suppressed. By a cleverly organized plot he was secretly captured, and at once publicly condemned and crucified, so that before his crowd of followers were aware of what had happened, their beloved leader had been killed in a way which at once made him accursed in the eyes of all good Jews. As the crafty priestly group had foreseen, in such a case the excitement of the mob cooled as quickly as it had heated, and Jesus was soon forgotten.

But the little group of simple people who constituted Jesus' inner circle of friends could not dismiss him from their minds. The light of their lives, for which they had deserted even their wives and children, had gone out, and the darkness of their despair was abysmal. They had been much changed by the life with their strangely powerful leader, and to go back to the old ways of living seemed a hopeless prospect. In grief they turned their faces from all their hopes to go the long journey back home to the lake of Galilee.

What happened historians do not know. It would seem that on the way, or shortly after their arrival, first Peter and then the others were transfixed at seeing Jesus apparently risen from the dead. Whatever the nature of their vision had been, their conviction that they had actually seen him turned into the most overwhelming religious experience. They rushed back to Jerusalem where the women of the party, who had remained in the city, shared their vision and the religious rapture it brought, until a large company, probably several hundred, were united in that most intense of all excitements, the excitement of a common religious experience. The origin of the Christian Church is quite unintelligible without taking account of this experience. Whatever its psychological interpretation, the fact that apparently uninteresting people can take fire and become irresistible under spiritual excitement is one of plainest facts of history. Such a spontaneous combustion of the spirit took place at Jerusalem as the culmination of the personal influence of Jesus, after the disciples believed they had seen him risen from the dead. And the fire that consumed them spread rapidly, as such fire usually does, in all directions.

THE FIRST CHRISTIANS

The company of about a hundred "enthusiastic" people, as they may well be called, who formed the first group of Christians in Jerusalem soon grew into a community of their own. They expected momentarily that Jesus would return to them from the skies, when he was going to recast all human society, and inaugurate the "Kingdom of God" on earth. In such an expectation possessions meant nothing to them; they pooled their money and goods, and lived all alike at a common table, from which baskets of food were carried to persons too ill or old to attend the common meal.

In Jerusalem there were found also Jews of another sort who had been regarding their scriptures and religion as the Way to the Spirit, in the Hellenistic sense already described. Some of these people too, after a time, fell under the influence of the rapturous enthusiasm of the Christians, and learned from them of this Jesus who had lived and gone back to heaven. To at least one of them, Paul, actually came the vision of the risen Jesus in heaven, and he, as possibly others before him, came to the epochal conclusion that Jesus was that very Spirit of God which a great number of men of the time have just been described as seeking. The Spirit, it seemed to Paul, had come down as the man Jesus to reveal the love and mercy of God; he had now returned to be with God and help men who wanted to be saved; while in a sense, since he was the universal Spirit, he was still here ready to enter into the heart of every man who desired him to do so. Seekers of the revelation of the Spirit might now shout Eureka!   In Christ, the Spirit of God, old things were done away, and all life filled with new hope and confidence.   Even the sacred Scriptures and religion of the Jews had now been surpassed, for while they were still a priceless guide, they had led, and could lead, men only a certain distance. Their work had now been completed by the coming of the Spirit itself, so that for old Judaism there was no longer any necessity. Freedom, the freedom of conformity to the Law of Nature or of God, which was the Spirit ruling this world, such freedom was no longer a dream but was actually to be had for the asking. So in the revelation of truth in Christ the problem of the late philosophy of Greece and Rome might be considered as having found a solution.   Christianity, or, as Paul and many of his successors called it, the perfect mystery religion, showed men the way to ultimate truth, showed them indeed Truth itself, and thereby the goal of philosophy as well as of religion was achieved.

This new version of the meaning of Jesus did not conquer the old without a struggle, but it fitted so precisely the needs of the age that it was not long before the Carpenter of Nazareth seems relatively to have been forgotten, so completely had he been everywhere transformed into the Christ-Spirit of the Church. Presented with such a Christianity Jews seem now to have been forced to make a choice: either they must give up their interpretation of Judaism as a Way to the Spirit in the sense of Hellenistic aspiration, or else they must accept Christ as the spiritualization of the old Law. Wherever the issue was presented the synagogues seem to have fallen into violent disagreement.

Members of the new faith had from the first been very active in trying to make converts. Convinced that the end of the age was imminent, they thought of nothing but to prepare themselves for the great event of Christ's return, and to get as many people ready along with themselves as possible. Missionaries went out in all directions. The most famous was Paul himself, who, sometimes with assistants, sometimes alone, travelled on the great open roads of the Empire from one metropolis to another. When he came to a city he would visit first the Jewish synagogue; then after the inevitable quarrel of the conservatives with those who were convinced by him he took most of the Gentile, that is, non-Jewish, visitors at the synagogue with his few Jewish converts and started a new group. As one such group became sufficiently grounded in the essentials of his message he pushed on to another city, there to repeat the same struggle. His adventures form one of the most thrilling odysseys of history, until at last he reached Rome itself, in chains, soon, if we may believe tradition, to be executed, but still confident, aggressive, dynamic. Paul was only one of the many, and in a surprisingly short time, thanks alike to Christian zeal and the ease of travel under the Roman administration, there were little Christian groups in every important center of the Empire. These groups, made up for the most part of Gentiles who had been interested in Judaism, were all regarded as hated outcasts by the Jews, and felt themselves not at all dependent upon the Jews.   Their teaching was full of ideas which they had taken over from Judaism, but their faces were turned toward the great pagan body of the Empire, as they brought a message that promised to solve the problems of the Gentile world.

The relation of this new Gentile Christianity to its ancestor Judaism is most difficult to define, and no one would have had more difficulty in depicting it than the early Christians themselves.   For sharply as Jews and Christians mutually repudiated each other, and much as Christianity turned to solving problems which were distinctively pagan rather than Jewish, Christianity yet took over several priceless characteristics from its original environment.   It had the Jewish Scriptures, of course, that superhuman source of truth. With these, like the Hellenized Judaism it had supplanted, it proposed to meet the Greek longing for salvation by a mystical knowledge.   Accordingly the early Christians found that the most appealing argument they could adduce either to Jews or Greeks consisted in quoting the Jewish Bible, and then by ingenious explanation demonstrating that the old books had accurately foretold details of the life of Jesus.   Further, Christianity took over from the Jewish religion its deep moral purpose, combined with the lofty ethical teaching of the Stoics.   Were the Greeks teaching that man should so school himself that he would ask little of life, and be happy under any misfortune?   The Christians took them at their word, and amazed the

Roman world by being able to live out such a doctrine, until, not an occasional individual, but groups of scores or hundreds at a time, sang hymns of joy in the terrible mines and prisons of the Romans, and even before the lions. It was a Jewish-Greek morality, Jewish in its patient steadfastness, Greek in its flouting of external goods, but still uniquely Christian in its emphasis upon love and humility, and in the abandoned enthusiasm with which it was practised.

And one other great thing Christianity had from Judaism: it had what has recently been called the sense of having a "cause" for which to live and die. Even at its height Græco-Roman philosophy was never optimistic that the world could be much improved; it encouraged the individual to live by high moral standards, but no change was ever looked for as a result in general social conditions. The buoyant clamor of the social reformer began with Christianity's new version of the Messianic social expectation of the Jews. For the Christian, like Christ, lived and died not for himself, but for the good of the world, to prepare society for the coming again of Christ when he should rule all men in a new kingdom of righteousness. It is in Christian literature that the word "hope" first, outside the Messianic writing of Jews, became social in its scope. And even when the earlier Jewish form of expectation of Christ's return began to fade into the indefinite future, Christians still believed that but for them the world would be destroyed by a wrathful God, that they were a leaven in the world, and that by their message the ills of humanity might definitely be removed.   While schools of philosophy had been only for the intelligent and scorned the multitude, while the mysteries had salvation exclusively for selected groups, Christianity had a message of eternal hope which it wanted to give to all men, high and low alike.

To plain people the simple Jesus who was also the savior Christ, and who was soon associated with his beautifully idealized mother, made a direct appeal of the sort they could understand.   To the philosophic mind the identification of Christ with the Spirit opened infinite possibilities of a spiritual philosophy, while it relieved men of the necessity of following that philosophy through intellectually, when, as often, they wanted to leap immediately to their goal.   Thus by loyalty to Christ men of all sorts seemed to find the solution of their problems here and hereafter to all eternity.   The longing of the Hellenistic Age had been satisfied.

THE FIRST SACRAMENTS

If Christianity began as a great rushing fire of enthusiasm at having discovered the meaning of life and freedom from its burden, it had another very important element.   Like the mystery religions, Christianity also, and from very early times, had sacred rites, two especially, whose sanctity had to be most rigidly guarded.   First, baptism was from the beginning the ceremony of initiation by which a convert was made a member of the Christian organization.   He was taken to a stream of running water and immersed in the stream while a sacred formula was spoken, at first "I baptize thee in the name of Jesus of Nazareth," but soon "I baptize thee in the name of the Father, and of the Son, and of the Holy Ghost." By this rite the convert was supposed to be washed pure from the guilt of his sins, and to have the center of his life so shifted by what they called "illumination," that is by the incoming of Christ's spirit, that thereafter not physical, but only spiritual, things mattered to him.

Still more sacred was the Eucharist. All early writers refer it back to an act of Jesus on the evening before he was arrested. At that time he took bread and broke it, and after a prayer, distributed portions to his disciples about the table, saying that it was his body. He then similarly blessed and caused each to drink from a cup of wine, which he called his blood. The earliest Christian communities, after their common meal, performed a ceremony in which this traditional act was rehearsed, and which from the first was regarded as the heart of Christian fellowship with one another, and as the great rite wherein the Christ-Spirit was again brought down in tangible form and imparted to the spirits of his followers. No one not baptized was allowed to share or even to witness the ceremony. Wherever Christianity spread, this custom always spread with it. In the subterranean tombs of Rome, in houses where Christians stealthily gathered by night in Asia Minor, this rite was the holy of holies of Christian worship. Indeed, by the early part of the second century, and perhaps earlier, Christians believed that the Eucharistic bread was "the flesh of our Savior

Jesus Christ, which suffered from our sins, and which the Father of his goodness raised up again," and that the wine was truly the blood which flowed from Jesus on the cross. No theory had yet been evolved to account for the transformation of the bread and wine into divine substance, but the reality of the change seems to have been widely accepted. Christianity had thus rejected polytheism and centered its aspiration upon a single, all-comprehensive deity. So by the secret rite of the Eucharist not *a* god, but the infinite God himself was not only represented, but by a miracle actually brought immediately present to the wondering hearts of the faithful. Here were ceremonies with possibilities of development almost unlimited, and yet which could be conducted under the humblest and most impoverished circumstances. For what rite has ever been devised more magnificently appealing than the breaking of the sacred bread together, the sharing of Christ's life in common, as it was done in prisons by little groups of Christians, with no ritualistic appurtenances, just before they went out singing into the arena to be torn by the wild beasts for their Savior?

THE GROWTH OF ORGANIZATION

It is obvious that as the Christians grew in number such sacred rites, particularly Eucharist, could be kept sacred only if there was a careful organization of the faithful to guarantee the manner and conditions of their rehearsal. Also, in a circle where the story of Jesus and his power to save had so rapidly grown, the story would tend to take on the most extravagant embellishments, which again only an efficient organization could check. The success of early Christianity, then, depended largely upon the ability of the Christians to produce a group of recognized leaders who would standardize and regulate Christian teaching and ritual. Early Christians seem with extraordinary prescience to have felt keenly the need of such organization, both local and general. The fact is all the more remarkable because no other religion of the Empire attempted to do more than organize locally. As we shall see, it was the fact that Christianity did have this genius for organization that, more than any other one thing, made it ultimately victorious over its rivals. Yet the beginnings of the great ecclesiastical system appear to have been simple and spontaneous enough.

The early Gentile communities had all been founded by travelling "apostles" or their helpers, and for a long time the scattered communities seem to have relied upon such men for their preachers. But while the preaching might be interrupted the local community life was continuous, and demanded some continuous organization. So in the earliest Christian records there are apparently two sorts of officials, the one a body of travelling evangelists, as we would call them now, the other the local officers of the congregation. The first sort were at that time usually called "prophets" or "apostles," and must have been interesting men. They were distinguished for "speaking in the spirit," which means that they went into a sort of trance or ecstasy from which, like the prophets at the seats of the ancient oracles, they poured forth the most impressive utterances. These prophecies, when uttered thus in the Spirit, it was a sin beyond all other sins for a Christian either to criticise or reject. We are fortunate in having still a very old manual, the *Teaching of the Twelve Apostles,* written not later than 125, perhaps much earlier, in which the early communities and their teachers and officers are described:

Receive anyone who comes to you teaching all those doctrines which we have described; if a teacher should turn aside and teach some other destructive doctrine, do not hear him; but if he teaches in a way to promote righteousness and knowledge of the Lord, receive him as the Lord. In regard to the prophets and apostles who teach according to the doctrine of the Gospel, let this be your rule: let every such apostle who comes to you be received as the Lord. But he may remain only one day, except in cases of emergency, when he may remain a second day. But if he remains three days, he is a false prophet. Furthermore, the apostle, when he leaves you, shall take nothing but bread sufficient to last until he reaches his next place of lodging. If he asks for money, he is a false prophet. You shall neither make trial of, nor judge, any prophet who speaks in the Spirit; for although all sins can be forgiven, this sin can not be forgiven. However, not every man who speaks in the Spirit is a prophet, but only those who live according to the Lord's moral standards. So then you shall distinguish between the false and the true prophets by their actions. As, for instance, no prophet, unless he is false, will eat of a meal which he may have ordered in the Spirit; and any prophet who teaches the truth, but does not practise it, is false. . . . And whosoever shall say in the Spirit, "Give me money," or give me anything else, is not to be heard; but if he shall bid you give for the needs of others, let no man judge him for that. . . . If he wants to take up his abode among you, and is an artisan, let him work for his living. If he has no trade, provide as well as you can that no idle Christian live among you. But if he will not so live, he is trying to make a profit from Christ. Beware of such people.

Besides these transient prophets, provision is made in the manual for occasional prophets who might settle in the Christian community, and be supported by contributions of food from the faithful. In addition to the prophets, who seem to have been almost entirely transient, the local organization had to have its own permanent officers. There seems to have been in each community a chief official, who was assisted by other men called "attendants" or "deacons." The chief official was interchangeably called a "bishop," which means in Greek the "shepherd" of the community, or "presbyter," a Greek word meaning "elder," and implying that he was the senior member of the congregation. Of the bishops and deacons the *Teaching of the Twelve Apostles* says:

Elect for yourselves bishops and deacons worthy of the Lord, meek and not avaricious, true men and tested. For they also do you the service of prophets and teachers. Do not despise them, for they are your honored ones, along with the prophets and teachers.

The greater respect seems here to be given to the travelling prophets who spoke in ecstasy, while the local bishops and deacons are of a less sacred character. But such was not permanently the case. The "prophetic gift," or power thus to speak from ecstasy, seems

early to have left the Church, and as it declined in frequency or favor the authority of the local bishops and
deacons rapidly increased.   From a very early time,
indeed, the prestige of all the officials in the congregation had been enormous.   At about the same time
as the writing of the *Teaching of the Twelve Apostles*
Ignatius urged his followers: "Be subject to the bishop,
and to one another, as Jesus Christ to the Father.
. . . We ought to look upon the bishop even as we
would upon the Lord himself."

APOSTOLIC SUCCESSION

During the second century the terms "presbyter"
and "bishop," at first interchangeable, came to be distinguished in such a way that only the head of the
chief congregation, in a district where several congregations were near together, was given the title
"bishop," while the heads of the smaller groups were
called "presbyters," or "priests."   In time this distinction came to be absolute, so that the bishop was regarded as being not only a higher official in the Church
than the priest, but also as a separate and distinct order
of ministry with powers which the priest did not share.
As this system had developed by the end of the second
century the power of the bishops over the lower clergy
had become so great that it is customary to speak of
the system as the "monarchical episcopate," which
means simply a system where the bishops have con-
trolling power over their subordinates.   And by this
time, strengthening the claims of the monarchical

bishops, there had developed the doctrine of the "Apostolic Succession" of these bishops. This conception, which had first been suggested in the beginning of the second century, or at the close of the first, was originally applicable to any head of a congregation, whether called bishop or priest. It represented the head of the congregation as deriving his authority not from being the oldest member of the congregation, nor from his having been elected by the congregation, but from his being the orderly successor in authority and spiritual power to the first Apostles. As each new man was elected to such an office it was believed that he should be installed in office by others who themselves had been installed by their predecessors in an unbroken chain back to the Apostles, who had been empowered for their work directly by Christ himself. Ordination, the ceremony of installation into office, was thus thought to pass on from one generation to the next the power of the Spirit originally given by Christ to the Apostles, and men who in their ordination had been given the peculiar office of receiving and using these powers were looked upon as of a different sort from the unordained, or laymen. But by the end of the second century not any head of a congregation, but only a bishop in the new sense, was believed to be able to transmit to others this apostolic power. Priests received the power when they were ordained, but not in such a way that they could create new priests. Only the bishops were the full successors of the Apostles. So when a new bishop was elected he must be consecrated by other bishops who in the consecration passed on this special power. It is very hard for those not reared in a Catholic environment to understand how reverently this succession of apostolic power came to be regarded. It was the very heart of the Church and of all human hopes. To keep in touch with the Divine Spirit of early Christianity men very early were taught and believed that they must be obedient to their bishops, keep "in communion" with them. For they thought that the life flow of Spirit came to men through their connection with this organization. The Church was the Body of Christ, the Vine of Christ; when an individual was severed from communion with the organization represented by the bishops he must expect to perish as a limb cut off from the body of a man or a tree.

This organization of the clergy protected the sacraments, as these sacred rites disseminating the spiritual life came to be called, by insisting that clergymen alone had the power properly to celebrate them; so in the Eucharist, for example, only when a priest or bishop consecrated the bread and wine did they change into vehicles of the Spirit of Christ. Very early in the second century Ignatius wrote:

Let that be deemed a proper Eucharist which is administered either by a bishop or by one to whom he has entrusted it. It is not lawful without the bishop either to baptize or to celebrate a love-feast (i.e. a Eucharist); but whatsoever he shall approve of, that is also pleasing to God, so that everything that is done may be secure and valid.

This was written so early that the distinction between the bishop and priest had not yet been made

clear. But from the time when the monarchical episcopate became recognized it was considered that the particular power passed on to the priest in ordination was
the power of consecrating the Eucharist. Everything
tended, then, to draw the Christian community together
into an ever closer feeling of unity with the bishops as
the dispensers of salvation.

While the succession of divine grace through the
bishops was thus coming to be regarded as the true
heart of Christianity another tendency was manifest in
the episcopate. The bishop who was at the head of a
large group of churches, or whose own church was in
a great city, rapidly came to be regarded with especial
reverence. Particularly was this true when the great
city was the original center of Christianity in a large
province, around which other churches, and even
bishoprics, had grown up as Christianity had expanded
from the center. The prestige of such a mother church
was rarely equalled by her daughters. And when, in
addition, the mother church had been founded by an
Apostle the preëminence of such an "Apostolic See" in
that section was beyond question. So Antioch, the
center from which Syria was Christianized; Corinth,
and Ephesus, where Paul himself had preached; Alexandria, which looked back only to Mark, but which
was the second city of the Empire, and early the intellectual center of Christianity; and above all Rome,
the capital of the Empire, and the traditional scene of
the martyrdoms of Peter and Paul; these great "sees,"
or bishoprics, had a most important prestige over the
ordinary bishoprics. Among the bishops themselves

there was much disputing over priority; for example Cyprian, a third century bishop of Carthage, fought the steadily growing prestige of Rome with all his power, and proclaimed the equality of all bishops. But his was a losing fight. Whatever the theory might be, the centering of authority in the great bishoprics was too natural and convenient for mere theories effectively to oppose it. By the beginning of the fourth century it had become clear that the bishops of Alexandria and Antioch easily dominated the east, and that Rome was unrivalled in the west.

So by Constantine's time the Church consisted of a large number of "sees" or "dioceses," in each of which was a number of local congregations. Each congregation was under the charge of a priest who had been ordained by the bishop at the head of the diocese. At the head of each diocese was a bishop, who governed the priests in the various congregations. The bishops were all theoretically of equal authority, but actually they regarded with great respect the authority of the bishop in the chief provincial city, and he in turn looked with practical subordination to the bishop at one of the two or three great centers of the Empire. No mystery religion had any such organization to unite and control the local congregations. It was this very effective organization which perhaps more than anything else attracted Constantine to Christianity. He had the cleverness to see that while the organization was quite informal in the sense that it was guaranteed by no constitution, and held together by no forcible discipline, it was yet a very real power. He perceived that if he could win the heads of the great Christian centers he would have the support of an institution which, like no other in the Empire, controlled the unswerving loyalty of an appreciable minority of his subjects of all classes and in all parts of the known world.

In addition to the constructive force of the spiritual fellowship of Christianity two influences were especially important in the cementing of the Church into a compact organization. The first was the inner struggle against heresy, or interpretations of Christianity repugnant to the majority of Christians, the second the persecution of the Christians by the Roman government. Of the former, details cannot here be discussed. The general tendency of early heresies was to go further than most Christians felt right in fitting Jesus Christ, as the Spirit Savior, into other schemes of salvation already at hand from oriental and Hellenistic theosophy, and to make Christ take a place as only one in a whole system of gods and spiritual powers. In a striking phrase of Dr. Bacon's, the great heresy of that day was not to make Jesus a man like any other man, but a god like any other god. Only the unique deity of Jesus could give Christianity any distinctive identity, so that in struggling against such heresy the Church was struggling to preserve its own existence, and was driven by necessity to draw up a set of rigid credal definitions, whose formulation, as we shall see, cost centuries of conflict; but without the creeds Christianity must have been absorbed in the great common melting pot of the Empire.

THE SCRIPTURES

One of the first needs in this struggle was for some written "Revelation" which was specifically Christian. The written authority for the earliest Christians had been the sacred books, or Bible, of the Jews which we now call the Old Testament. To it early Christian teachers had appealed to support all their teachings. But while salvation through Jesus could be read back into the Old Testament by adroit interpretations of various statements in the Old Testament, the Christians found to their sorrow that the same methods could be used to justify what they considered the rankest heresies and blasphemies. It was essential to find some written authority for Christianity which could be understood in its plain literal sense. Such books could not well be made to order, for books written by contemporaries are always subject to contemporary criticism. The writings of the Apostles, then, and the books supposedly written directly under their supervision, gradually came to be the new Bible of Christianity, which was used in conjunction with the Old Testament, and which checked inconvenient interpretations of the Old Testament. About most of the writings which now form the New Testament there was little question. The writings of Paul, the older lives of Jesus bearing the names of Apostles or apostolic followers, the "Prophecies" dictated by the Spirit, were early treasured as of unique value for Christian instruction. These books got general recognition among the Christians at first as they came to be read publicly in the formal services of the churches along with the Old Testament. Custom varied in different churches, but gradually some books earlier used locally were discarded, and quite informally the majority of the books came everywhere to be agreed upon. A few books were much more disputed, so that not until the fifth century was the "canon," or list of writings regarded as of apostolic authority for Christians, considered to be finally closed. At the same time the authority of these books was likewise gradually increasing. At first they were preserved simply as priceless relics of the early period, but were not regarded as of equal authority with the Old Testament. In the middle of the second century they were used as other historical records are used, as witnesses to events of the past. But a century later it came to be believed that they were "inspired" in the same way in which the Old Testament was "inspired." They thus furnished the needed body of revealed Christian truth, which, when used with the Jewish Scriptures as a single inspired Bible, had manifold uses. With it heresies could be confuted and an active propaganda be carried on among heathen neighbors who, it has been seen, were eager to hear about inspired literature which told of salvation. So the Church acquired her literary foundation which she had created, and whose meaning she could alone authoritatively explain.

PERSECUTION

The attacks from within Christianity upon her doctrines which, while costing her many losses, tended to unite the faithful in ever closer bonds of thought and sympathy, were simultaneous with attacks from without. For from the first Christianity was viewed with suspicion by the government officials. The chief reasons for this antipathy were, first, a fixed notion in all non-Christian circles that the Christians, while they pretended to peculiar virtue, were actually practising in their secret meetings the most horrible acts of incest and murder, and even of cannibalism; second, a suspicion of the Christians, from the very fact that they met in secret to celebrate the Eucharist, that, éven worse than committing immoralities, they were plotting against the government. This suspicion was given poignancy by the fact that the Christians refused, in their zeal against idol-worship, to observe the apparently very harmless custom of dropping a pinch of incense upon the incense-burner before the Emperor's statue. To the ordinary citizen this act meant no more than saluting the flag does today; it was merely a gesture by which one declared his patriotism. But the Roman Empire had deified its Cæsars, and Christians felt that to burn incense to them was to deny their faith in the one Lord Jesus Christ. A sect which would refuse so simple a gesture of patriotism was given then as little patience as a modern crowd in war time would

extend to a fanatic who in a patriotic mass-meeting refused to salute the flag with the others.

Still more obvious an indication of the undesirability
of Christianity in Roman eyes was the fact that its converts were drawn in an overwhelming majority from the
lowest classes of society. Then as now the governing
classes were apprehensive of a movement which
brought into a closely knit and secret organization the
servants and slaves of society. At that time Christianity was regarded by an upper-class Roman much
as an upper-class American would regard a society
which united for secret meetings and eternal brotherhood the lowliest toilers of America, which, it was
universally believed, made incest and murder a regular
part of its meetings, and whose members refused to
salute the flag, and, in most cases, to serve in the army.
In an age when torture of unfortunate people was the
great popular form of entertainment furnished by the
government, it can hardly be a matter of surprise that
the cry was frequently raised that such people be
thrown to the lions. It was already by the end of the
first century a capital crime to confess oneself a Christian, and as such it was regarded consistently by strict
legalists until the Edict of Toleration in 313.

But actually the persecutions of the first two centuries, while persistent and always imminent, were
sporadic and largely local. Indeed, with the exception
of a decade of persecution under Marcus Aurelius
(about 170-180), the Christians lived in steadily
diminishing danger, and while they were never entirely
safe, in many places they were able to practise their

religious rites openly and with impunity.   But in the year 248 a mob outburst in Alexandria against the Christians was taken up systematically by the new Emperor Decius, and for two years the Christians throughout the Empire were subjected to an organized movement to force them to sacrifice to the gods.   Both Gallus and Valerian in turn carried out the policy of Decius, so that from 249-259 Christians were harassed by a fearful persecution in which many of their number were killed or banished, and in which all church property was confiscated.   Because of the stubborn resistance of the Christians against all efforts to make them give up their religion, only the strong emperors attempted to enforce the laws against them.   Valerian's son Gallienus, a worthless weakling, gave up the struggle and restored their lands to the Christians.   Practical toleration as this was, it was not an official toleration, for all the laws were allowed to stand against them, and it needed only a strong ruler for the trouble to break out afresh.   But strong rulers were scarce in the decadent period of Rome, and it was not until the reign of Diocletian in 303 that the Christians were again molested on a large scale.

From the failure of the persecution of 249-259 the Church emerged stronger than ever.   Bonds forged in the furnace of suffering are the strongest human nature knows, and all that the persecution had succeeded in doing was to transform the iron links of church organization into the hardest steel.   During the period which followed, it became the most powerful organization in the Empire, and united probably about one-

tenth of the population of the entire Roman world into
a solid body, whose face had been turned in opposition
to the Empire by the persecutions. Not that Christians
were not exemplary subjects. They were peaceful and
law-abiding, but they had made the choice repeatedly
between the Empire and their religion, and everyone
understood that upon occasion they would do so again.

VICTORY

By a strong ruler like Diocletian, who was trying
to get the whole Empire under the control of the government, such a situation could not be tolerated. Because the Christians refused to comply with the religious forms of the government, and so set themselves up as potential rebels, the Empire must either
surrender to Christianity in order to secure the alliance
and assistance of the Church, or else it must destroy the
Church utterly. Diocletian was not a man who surrendered easily, and consequently he declared war on the
Christians. He was helped by those who wanted to
gain the lands which he confiscated from the Church,
but in general public feeling toward the Christians was
much more kindly now than in the time of Decius. As
a result the persecution was very uneven, and varied in
intensity with the views of the local governors. When
Diocletian retired in 305 it ceased entirely in the west,
though the new Emperor in the east, Galerius, continued to harass the Christians with unmitigated
hatred. But he was engaged in a struggle in which
failure was inevitable, and when the aspirants in the

west, Constantine and Licinius, wished to surrender to Christianity in order to get the support of the great Christian organization, Galerius also gave in and joined them in an Edict of Toleration for the Christians. When Galerius shortly afterwards had died, and Constantine had conquered the Roman world, he renewed with Licinius the policy of toleration for Christians in the great Edict of Milan, late in the year 312, or early in 313. Constantine did not himself become a member of the Church until just before his death, and Christianity did not become the state religion to the total exclusion of paganism until 395. But the favor which Constantine showed Christians throughout his life made it the court religion, and consequently the Edict of Toleration of 312 or 313 is regarded as closing the first epoch of the history of Christianity. Thereafter the Church was not primarily a persecuted body of earnest followers of Christ, but a great organization of the Roman Empire. In the Church there survived much of the beautiful spirit of the early followers of Jesus, but that spirit no longer dominated the whole. No religion has ever been able long to keep its exalted idealism untarnished in a time of prosperity; the Christian Church under Constantine and his successors made no exception to the rule.

CHAPTER II

THE STATE CHURCH OF THE ROMAN EMPIRE

CONSTANTINE AND THE CHURCH

ALTHOUGH only about one-tenth of the citizens of the Empire were Christians, Constantine recognized in the Christian brotherhood a cohesive force with which nothing else in the Empire could compare. For the feeling of Christian brotherhood was not only widespread: it had already expressed itself in an organization which claimed a monopoly of this thing which all Christians seemed to prize more than life, the saving grace of Christ which it gave them in the sacraments. In all parts of the Empire were local organizations of this one Catholic Church, and everywhere it was admitted that the local organization had validity only as it remained in organic connection with the Church universal. Could not the loyalty to the Church be so guided as to become loyalty also to the Empire? Constantine thought that this could be done if he tolerated Christianity, and if, by taking an official interest in its discipline, he encouraged the clergy to strengthen its organization. That is, he hoped by making the Church a part of the state that he could tap the abundant Christian store of spiritual strength to supply his sadly enervated Empire. So, unlike Diocletian,

Constantine, as has been seen, threw his mantle of protection and favor over the delighted Christians.

With this hope of strengthening the Empire by using the organization of the Church went another motive in Constantine's toleration of the Church, namely superstition. From earliest times, one of the chief functions of an officer in the Roman state had been to keep the gods favorably disposed toward Rome and her projects. Always the Romans had said that if they were more successful than their enemies in war it was because the Romans were more skilful in attracting the divine favor. At a time when matters went badly for the Romans they had accordingly always turned to religion as the hope for better success, in which case they not only increased their rigor in observing their own traditional rites, but frequently sought out new deities and rites, the recognition of which might "change their luck." Now for a long time matters had indeed been going badly for the Empire, and Constantine seems sincerely to have hoped that by tolerating the Christians he might get the support of their deity and so be more successful. The Christians assured him that it would be so, and when he tried putting their symbol with the symbols of other religions carried by the army he won a great victory. According to the logic of a vigorous and practical Roman of the day it would indeed be foolish to antagonize further a people who had such possibilities of support in their organization, and who worshipped a victory-bringing deity.

Yet the Church could serve Constantine's purpose only if it were kept united in organization and spirit.

Hence from Constantine's time matters of Christian doctrine and discipline were affairs of state. For with the state and Church coöperating, in so far as heresies or disputes about administration threatened to dismember the Church they would weaken the state also, so that if the state were to be helped rather than injured by her alliance with the Church, the emperors must intervene to settle controversies about orthodoxy and ecclesiastical practice which it is now hard to understand as issues of practical statecraft. At the same time the more the emperors gave their attention to the Church, the more political they made its organization. The result, as will be seen, was quite different in the east from that in the west. In the east the Church finally settled down as a department of the state. In the west, because of the collapse of the state, the Church went forth into the storms of early mediæval civilization with its head fogged with half-formed dreams of universal political supremacy. In the west, indeed, one is presented with the stupendous spectacle of the death of the greatest organization the world had ever seen, and the reincarnation of its spirit in an organization at least as magnificent. For the spirit of the Empire became the spirit of the Church. In this chapter this transformation will be discussed in connection with the legal and administrative aspects and ambitions of the Empire. The next chapter will be concerned with the effect of the Empire and its life upon other aspects of the Church.

It has already been stated that strong as was the feeling of union among Christians in the face of pagan opposition, and cohesive as their organization appeared in comparison with the weakening bonds of Roman society, the Church as a whole was actually far from being a close-knit organization.   In theory there could be but one Church, the seamless robe, the single body of Christ.   All admitted this, and yet the immediate difficulty in Constantine's time was that when any difference of opinion arose on which the churches in various regions took different sides there was no way in which the Church as a whole could speak so that all Catholics would at once recognize her decision as final. It was easy to keep the feeling of the one Catholic Church when a generally united sentiment was opposed by scattered heretics.   But when whole sections, with their bishops and priests, were convinced that other whole sections were completely in the wrong, what should be done?   For the Church had a two-fold obligation: first to transmit the grace of Christ in sacraments through the apostolic succession, and second to preserve the true doctrine.   The Church was not the Church at all unless it fulfilled both functions.   Consequently large sections tended recurrently to drop away according as they felt that the rest of the faithful were failing in either particular.   The Church which Constantine took over was threatened with dismemberment on both accounts, and accordingly he was compelled, if the Church was to be a force for unity, to try to settle the disputes.

In the matter of Church practice, that is in the matter of preserving and administering the sacraments, there had developed a very serious controversy as a result of a disputed election to the office of Bishop of Carthage. Two men claimed to have been properly elected, and local councils or synods were quite unable to settle the matter. One of the claimants, Cæcilian, was recognized by the rest of the Church, but his famous rival, Donatus, undaunted, defied the Church as being corrupt if it could recognize one elected by such methods as he thought had put his opponent into office. He said that since he and his followers alone stood for purity of election, and so of apostolic succession, they were the only remnant of the true Church of Christ. It was precisely the sort of argument by which the majority had frequently expelled undesired minorities; now a powerful minority had turned its back upon the majority, and the Church as a whole had no way once and for all to pronounce it wrong. Had there been such a way at the beginning, the whole affair would have amounted to nothing. As it was it had dragged on for some years by the time Constantine began to take official interest in the Church, and was a great source of weakness in all the provinces of North Africa and Spain.

Constantine at once recognized the importance of settling this particular dispute and of getting some sort of machinery by which the Church could act as a whole. His first move was to ask the Bishop of Rome to call a synod to arbitrate the matter. Only a few bishops attended, however, so that its declaration for Cæcilian helped not at all. Constantine next tried to get an expression of opinion from the entire Church under his supervision. (He was then Emperor only in

the west, with his capital at Milan.)   He commanded
as an imperial act that the bishops of his realm as-
semble in Arles.   This council met in 314, and ratified
the findings of the previous Synod of Rome, but at its
close the bishops dared not return until they had Constantine's permission to do so.   The Donatists then
appealed to the Court of the Emperor himself, where
they finally lost their suit and were threatened with
imperial discipline if they continued to resist.   But
they returned unconvinced to Africa where they survived until extinguished by the Vandals a century and
a half later.   Apparently nothing had been settled, and
yet the results were very real.   For under Constantine
the entire Christian sentiment of the west had been for
the first time brought to bear upon a problem, an
official pronouncement had been made, and if the result
for the Donatists was not convincing, the effect in
uniting the Church as a whole was profound.

THE ARIAN CONTROVERSY

From the point of view of doctrine a still greater
problem faced Constantine.   In the latter part of the
third century a new dispute had arisen as a larger
number of Christians were men of philosophical training who wanted to fit their worship of Christ into the
prevailing philosophical system of the day.   The difficulties in doing so centered about the question, "In
what sense was Christ divine?"   For true deity was, by
all accepted definition at the time, best to be thought
of as bare Unity, which was utterly different from all

the complications of this life. God had no parts, no constitution, no emotions. He was always active in thinking, but in no other way, and indeed He was nothing but Mind in its most abstract form. He seems to have been a glorification of the vanishing point of perspective, the resolution and orientation of everything in the world, and yet completely unrelated to anything outside of Himself.

The problem was, how, if God was such a Unity, could Jesus of Nazareth be divine also. The early solution had been to identify Christ with the Spirit which radiated out of God, and which had created and now governs the world. Practically, Christ was the Christians' God, to whom they prayed as the devotees of Mithra prayed to Mithra, and little attention was paid to the deity of philosophy. Such a solution had satisfied the first two centuries of Christians, but did not answer at all when people of philosophic training were converted. From the middle of the third century the question had been raised with increasing insistence: if Christ was the incarnate Word or Spirit, in what sense was he divine; was he truly God, or demi-god? Early in the fourth century the issue was brought out sharply by Arius, a brilliant churchman in Alexandria, who became the protagonist of the philosophical party by openly arguing that if Jesus was the incarnate Word of God he must be subordinate to God, a radiation out from God, divine, but still not true deity. Against him Alexander, the venerable bishop of Alexandria, led the group primarily interested in the religious tradition of Christianity. He was later succeeded by Athanasius as bishop and party leader, so that this party, in contrast to the Arian party, came to be called the Athanasian, or, as it was ultimately victorious, the Orthodox party. The dispute became most complicated. The Arian party adopted the formula that the nature of Christ was divine, but was "different" from God's nature, for God's nature could not suffer any division or external relationships. On the other hand the Athanasian party, since their interest was primarily the religious glorification of Christ, insisted that, philosophy or no philosophy, Jesus Christ had the true divine nature, exactly the "same" nature as God Himself. They felt obliged to refuse any compromise on this position because they had come to hope for their own immortality by being deified, and the way in which they expected to become deified themselves was by partaking, in the Eucharist, of the body of Christ who was fully God.

That is, in the titanic struggle over what seems a minute and unimportant detail the point at issue was not so much the formula itself as the great question as to whether the philosophy and science of the day was to be made fundamentally nonsensical to make room for the demands of a mystery theory in religion, or the religious momentum behind the mystery theory would suffer itself to be guided to fit into contemporary science. Was man to take faith or reason for his guide in the future? The outcome of such a conflict could not long be in doubt. For centuries the Græco-Roman mind had been losing its vigor, and was increasingly ready to take the easiest path to repose.

Those who were finding their peace of mind in the God Christ had a confidence which the enfeebled philosophical spirit of the late Empire could not hope to resist. Indeed it was but a short time until the Arian party in the Church had compromised its position, and was defending the statement that Christ was of a "similar" nature to God's, rather than that he was of a "different" nature. But this concession, while it did not satisfy the Athanasians whose formula was that Christ had the "same" nature as God, was philosophically just as meaningless, so that in defending it the Arian party ceased to have any real philosophical significance. Consequently the great struggle between this and the orthodox party throughout the fourth century was almost entirely a political affair, with simply the sort of rivalry for public favor with which we are too familiar in America, with no real issue between the parties. To one who tried to be true to philosophical thought, as did the Emperor Julian, for example, in the middle of the fourth century, each party seemed as absurd as the other, and the whole struggle appeared to be only a competition for offices and money. Yet it is possible that in that period of degeneration no more fortunate thing could have happened than the shaping of the great Christian formulæ out of the ruins of Greek thought, and the preservation thereby of at least some of the points of view of the past to be the guide of subsequent centuries.

To Constantine, who cared nothing for the merits of the controversy, the situation presented only the problem of how he was to unite the Church on either one

side or the other in order to get the support of the
Church's unified force.   When news of the trouble
reached him he drew up an appeal in a letter addressed
in common to both Alexander and Arius which he sent
by his most intimate clerical friend, Bishop Hosius of
Spain.   Constantine pointed out that the question in
dispute was one which human minds could never settle,
and a dispute which was in any case a matter of minor
detail, for both sides still agreed in what seemed to
him the main points, that is in matters of morality and
worship.   He reminded them that in philosophical sects
the philosophers often disagreed in details, but still
remained together because of what they had in common, while they respected each other's differences of
opinion on smaller matters.

Clearly Constantine had no appreciation of the importance of the question in the minds of the disputants
at this early stage, so that his letter belittling their
dispute only embittered both sides.   His next expedient
was therefore to try to repeat his success at Arles by
again settling a Church controversy at a Council held
under the awe of imperial prestige.   In 325 he summoned to Nicea all the bishops of the east, including
many groups hardly recognized by the orthodox, with
a generous representation of western bishops, including, of course, Rome.   For two months a fierce battle
raged.   The extremists on one side, led by Arius,
seemed totally given over to the philosophical implica-
tions of the terms in question, and openly expressed
their unconcern if proof-texts from the Scriptures could
be quoted against them.   Extremists on the other side

were well represented by one loyal, though uneducated Christian who reproved those who relied upon reason, and said that Christ and his apostles did not teach dialectics, cleverness or subtleness, but simple-mindedness as preserved in faith and good works. The majority of the assembly, however, fell between these two extremes, and tried to use both the authority of Scripture and rational argument. The Emperor sat in his golden chair as umpire through the entire two months of argumentation and eventually all but five of the more than three hundred bishops present agreed on a formula. The final settlement was a complete victory for the party of Alexander and Athanasius. A creed was adopted containing their chosen phrase "of the same nature as the Father," and Arius with all his sympathizers was not only condemned by the Church, but banished from the Empire, while an Imperial Decree made it an offense to be punished by immediate death if any man should ever try to harbor in secret a book written by Arius.

Apart from its dogmatic interest, quite apparently the Council marks a definite step beyond Constantine's first attempt at Arles in uniting the church by imperial discipline. The Council was not only summoned by imperial decree, but the expenses of travel and entertainment were paid from the imperial treasury, and its proceedings were supervised throughout by imperial authority. At the end the decisions of the Council became imperial law by receiving the confirmation of the Emperor. The effect of this precedent was enormous in all future ages of the Church. Whatever the religious origin of the Christian Faith, the Church as a universal corporation was formed deliberately as a branch of secular government and the first expressions of the Church as a whole were matters at the same time of faith and of imperial legislation. Thereafter, as the organization of the Church steadily became stronger, it always looked to the forces of government for coercive power.

THE CHURCH ACQUIRES POLITICAL POWER

Constantine also established important precedents in his treatment of the clergy. In pagan Rome, the clergy, what few there were, had certain outstanding privileges. Since their office often involved large personal expenditure, they were exempt from all state financial obligations and from the necessity of military service. These privileges Constantine extended to the great body of Christian clergy, which in fact accorded them official standing as individuals in the Empire. For the basis of exemption of priests in the early days of Rome had been the fact that they were regarded as representatives of the state in its dealings with those gods who had been officially elected as such by the senate. The priests were hence officials of the state, and not to be disturbed in their beneficent public service. In giving to Christian clergy the same privileges, Constantine laid the foundation of the political independence of the clergy which later provoked centuries of controversy. Similarly Constantine recognized as legal the courts of the bishops. During times of persecution, when Christians had a matter to settle, it had rarely been wise to appeal to a Roman court. The custom had arisen, following the earliest Christian advice, of appealing such disputes to the bishop as final judge. The decisions of the bishops Constantine now recognized as of final validity, quite on a par with the decisions of the imperial courts. A case might be taken before either an ecclesiastical or an imperial court according to the desires of the contestants. Also, Constantine recognized the Church as a valid property-holding institution. Legally regarded now as a corporation under the state, each episcopal seat was allowed to hold property, and was frequently given by the state money and land, or former pagan temples, to be kept as Church property. As part of this policy, Constantine permitted people to bequeath their property to the Church, a privilege the clergy were not slow to urge the pious wealthy to exercise. Land once in the possession of the Church practically never left its hands, so that by 370 the landed wealth of the Church had already become a vexing problem and continued so until modern times.

Under Constantine there began also an attempt to fit the Church into the new divisions of the Empire. Diocletian and Constantine had established four great prefectures in the Empire, subdivided into dioceses, each diocese in turn made up of several provinces. At the chief city, or metropolis, of each province it now seemed desirable to establish formally a Metropolitan Bishop, or Metropolitan, who would supervise all the bishops of the province. In turn the bishop in the

great capital city of a diocese was to have similar
supervision over the metropolitans in the various provinces of the diocese.   There was at first no particular
title for such Diocesan-Bishops, but they came gradually to be known as Patriarchs.   The arrangement was
of course an expression of the Roman desire for cen-
tralized control by means of a systematic organization,
but it was never fully worked out.   In places where a
political capital of a diocese, such as Alexandria, had
already been associated with episcopal prestige over
all provincial bishops and metropolitans, the system
could at once be installed, as was done in the case of
Alexandria by the Nicene Council.   Antioch, Rome,
Carthage, and soon Constantinople, were also obvious
ecclesiastical capitals.   But though the system could
never be put into operation as a whole, the very fact
that it was regarded as the ideal did much to bind the
state and Church together in men's minds.

So much space has been given to the treatment of
the Church by Constantine because the generation
flourishing in the first half of the fourth century saw
a transition in the Christian Church comparable in its
importance only to that change from a Palestinian
sect to a mystery religion of salvation witnessed by the
first generation of Christians.   During the first three
hundred years, Christianity had flourished as a religious body made up of people who at considerable
risk to themselves joined an organization held together
only by the devotion of its members.   But Constantine's desire to use the organization for his political
ends had introduced problems totally unknown to the

earlier Christians. Church discipline had now become
a matter of legal enforcement. Heresy was a crime
against the state, to be punished by banishment or even
execution. The decrees of the Church councils were
made into formal imperial law by the sanction of the
Emperor. Accordingly, where the Church had for-
merly been, in its relation to paganism at least, interested in religious liberty, this interest now turned into
active persecution by Christians of those, at first especially the heretics, who did not accept her decrees.
And almost at once the Emperor came to be regarded
as having the final word even in matters of doctrine.
The new spirit went down through every part of the
Church. Whereas a bishop had heretofore been, with
few exceptions, one who held his office with slight
financial return, and often great risk, he was now an
important Roman official, conducting a recognized law
court, frequently managing large financial estates, and
prone to dispute his rights step by step against the
other officials of the state. It was thus natural that in
a period of steady decline of state power the Church
would take over more and more of the business of
government, until, at the complete collapse of the state
it would begin to dream of being itself the ideal rulership for the world, though such a thought was utterly
foreign to the Church of the first three centuries.

THE TURBULENCE OF THE FOURTH CENTURY

The weakness of this new union of Church and
state was evident from the beginning. If the Church

was to have become a unified organization under the Emperors, the Emperors themselves should have been consistent in their attitude toward problems of the Church. Constantine and his followers made the fatal mistake of doctrinal instability and inconsistency. Three years after Constantine had promulgated the decrees of Nicæa and banished the leading Arians, he came under the personal influence of certain Arians and immediately changed his attitude. While still preserving the creed of Nicæa as the official creed of the Church, he restored to their former positions all Arians who had been degraded, while one of the ablest, Eusebius, Bishop of Cæsarea, the learned historian of the Church, became his intimate friend. Fresh synods were held, many of which drew up purely Arian creeds, and Arius himself was so favorably regarded that by command of Constantine he was to have been given communion in the cathedral of Constantinople, a sign of his complete acceptance at the most important center of Christianity. The cathedral church was spared this "ignominy," for on the day before the ceremony Arius is said to have died in a sudden contortion which burst open his bowels. To the modern mind, as to Gibbon, the faithful had clearly saved their faith by the use of poison, but of course in ecclesiastical records the instance was described as a miraculous intervention of God for the purity of the Church. The intrusion of the state in doctrinal matters to insure the unity of the Church had indeed only intensified the division, for it rallied the followers of both sides to focus their influence upon an Emperor who cared so little for the merit of the case as to change his mind with most bewildering frequency.

If Constantine produced confusion and demoralization in the church by his indecision, his son Constantius worked havoc. Constantius was an avowed sympathizer with the Arians, yet took incredible pleasure in encouraging the disputes of various party representatives, and was enormously amused in attempts at drawing up creeds of all kinds to fit various opinions. During his reign, as during his father's, synods large and small were being held almost constantly in various parts of the Empire, until Ammianus, a pagan, complained that even the imperial posting system was thrown out of joint by the troops of bishops galloping on the roads in all directions to and from such assemblies. In the synods no trick from slanderous defamation and bribery to murder was too base to be employed by either side to gain its ends. Whatever merits the dispute had had at the beginning, the question in the end became purely a party matter, not the least of whose protagonists were the eunuchs and concubines of the court.

On one occasion the "orthodox" Constans, Constantius' brother, threatened Constantius with civil war if the orthodox protagonist, Athanasius, was not restored to his bishopric at Alexandria. But when this danger had passed and Constantius again wished to exile Athanasius he could only do so by sending an army and navy to attack Alexandria, for the power of Athanasius far surpassed the authority of the state officers in that city. A frightful siege and sack resulted,

with the city exposed for four months to the licentious-
ness and greed of a hostile army.

Violence was common everywhere. In a dispute
over election to the See of Rome riots arose between
Arians and orthodox in which over three thousand
people were killed. The Arian candidate was tem-
porarily successful. Accordingly he forced the orthodox into accepting sacraments from his party by prying
their mouths open with a block of wood while the
sacred wafer was pushed down their throats. The
Arians persuaded orthodox women to be baptised by
flogging them, or by even more brutal methods of
torture. From the African desert to the Black Sea
armies were marching and in the name of God razing
villages, murdering, and looting. Clearly the assumption by the Emperor of power to settle ecclesiastical
disputes had worked not for the union but the division
of both the Church and state.

JULIAN THE APOSTATE

It is not difficult to understand the reaction of a
character like Julian, who in 360 succeeded Constantius, to such a situation as this. He had as a
youth been carefully trained by Christian teachers, but
on maturity had come to regard all Christianity
theologically as but a travesty of philosophy and eccle-
siastically as a political menace. He desired, therefore, to disengage the state from all its entanglements
with Christianity, and to return to the Edict of Milan,
by which the Christian religion was tolerated beside

paganism, but with paganism as the official religion. It is to be remembered that the Christian Church had never yet been formally made the religion of the Roman state to the exclusion of all other worship. But in Constantius' day the court had been entirely Christian of one sort or the other and it had even been made a capital offense to sacrifice to any god, though the law could never have been generally enforced. Christians had been encouraged to appropriate heathen temples or were given them outright, so that Christianity could be regarded practically as the state religion. Really only a legal formalism was left to distinguish between ecclesiastical and imperial politics. All this Julian felt must be changed. As an educated gentleman he regarded with horror the shocking quarrels between Christians, and rightly decided that whatever had been the merits of the case at the beginning, in the course of the controversy both sides had long forfeited any claim to support. As he saw it the Christians were slaughtering not only those who had been faithful to paganism, "but also men who are as much astray as yourselves, heretics, because they do not wail over the corpse (i.e. Jesus) in your own particular fashion." Since Christianity had had no official status, but based its prestige only on the patronage of the last three Emperors, as soon as a pagan Emperor appeared its standing at once was changed. Julian stripped from the Christian clergy all their new legal powers. Bishops were no longer recognized as valid judges in civil affairs, the right to receive legacies was taken from the Church, and clergymen were subject to taxation like other citizens of the Empire. The clergy were not to be supported in their attempts to stir up rebellion against these decrees on pain of imperial punishment. Julian did not encourage the pagans to turn the tables and attempt to coerce Christians to become pagan. He thought this beneath the dignity of paganism and its gods. If the madmen wanted to worship in their own way, let them go unharmed in their folly. For to drag such blasphemers to the altars of the gods would be a profanation of the sacred places.

But when Julian began to express his ideas as to what should be the true religion he showed the weakness of the decadent paganism he was defending. He tried uncritically to keep practically everything that had come from classical antiquity, along with many of the innovations from heathen Persia and Egypt. The mysteries of Mithra and Isis received his devout support, and he cherished the traditional worship of Roman deities along with the myths of Homer and Hesiod. He did not revere the philosophers of all schools equally, but he respected them all highly, while the late Platonism or Neo-Platonism, which had been developing at the same time as Christianity, he attempted to make the philosophical background of his hopeless mixture of ideas from the past. The result was as unreasoned and unsatisfying as the most unreflecting Christian oratory, while it lacked the great force which carried Christianity relentlessly forward, its profound spiritual conviction.

The impression one gets from the writings of Julian is that his real objection to Christianity was esthetic.

He loved the poetry of old paganism, while he abhorred the excesses of party janglings, and was shocked at Christian treatment of philosophical terminology. But much as he disliked Christianity he had nothing so good as a whole to offer in its place. His reign lasted for but three years, when he fell in battle with the traditional cry, "Thou hast conquered, O Galilean." The tradition is probably not authentic, but it is one of those remarks which should have been made if it actually was not. For at the fall of Julian, with whose name was ever thereafter hissed the terrible nick-name Apostate, there collapsed the last attempt of delirious classicism to rise from its deathbed. Rightly did the generation of Julian feel that if it wanted the comfort of a divine salvation, nothing comparable to Christianity had ever been available. Julian's successor restored to the Church the privileges Julian had taken away, and no ancient or medieval Emperor thereafter dared or cared to oppose Christianity as a religion again. Toleration more or less grudging was allowed to paganism for another thirty years, but then ceased altogether at the definite declaration in 395 by Theodosius that the Empire was a Christian state to the exclusion, and abolition, of all heathenism. The rites of various local gods continued privately to be observed long afterwards, particularly in the country districts, but subject to the disapproval of all constituted authorities.

THE TRINITY AND INCARNATION

So far as the Church itself was concerned, the in-difference of Julian helped very much in the solution of its problems. The Emperors who thought to save the Empire by adding to it the mysterious strength of Christianity had utterly failed in their attempt by their own lack of settled and intelligent policy. Instead of uniting the Church the Emperors had patronized first one side and then the other in her internal quarrels, until both sides had a strength otherwise impossible. It was only by the Church's lapsing into her former independence that the issue fell to its proper propor-tions, and could approach a settlement. As has already been stated, the reason why Arianism with the support of the militant Constantius failed to vanquish the Nicene Creed was that the Arians were themselves divided as to what they wanted in its place, while the orthodox party stood united upon a definite platform. Now when political support failed to rally the Arians, the only united party in the field was that of the ortho-dox which at once began to gain strength from all sides. A succession of mildly orthodox Emperors followed Julian until in 380 Gratian and Theodosius took the matter in hand, called the great synod of Constanti-nople of 381, and confirmed, permanently, the Nicene Creed. By this time the issue had been complicated by the added problem of the standing of a third Divine Person, the Holy Spirit, which had begun as a variant name for the Word of God incarnate in Christ, but which had gradually come to be thought of as an additional divine person. The Holy Spirit was associated with the Son, so that at the synod of Constantinople the orthodox doctrine of the Trinity was affirmed for all time. The solution as it finally was evolved declared for one divine Nature (which Nature was a mystery), representing itself simultaneously in three Persons, the Father, Son, and Holy Spirit. Each of these was fully God, and yet there were not three natures, not three Gods, but one Nature and one God. Yet the Persons were not simply phases of a single Being, but distinct Persons. That is, the solution of the problem of how the one deity of contemporary science could be truly spoken of in the case of more than one person had been made by a perfectly meaningless paradox. In mathematical language, which is quite as applicable as the terms manufactured or distorted from their proper meanings for the formulation of this dogma, if x represents the Divine Nature, the equation for the Trinity is $x = 3x$. But the doctrine was raised beyond irreverent protest by the assertion that this seemingly impossible statement was made possible by the mysterious nature in this case of x, a nature quite beyond the discovery or comprehension of human minds.

Still, little as the solution had to offer to an intellectual seeker for truth, Christianity preserved thereby its great religious contribution to the world. That God was at once the ultimate principle of the world in the sense of science of whatever school; that at the same time He was a personal presence in the world, guiding men, loving men, and accessible to men's prayers, even having revealed Himself and suffered in order to draw men to a higher life; and yet that there was not a family of Gods but one God: this is what the formula of the Trinity succeeded in crystallizing. Of answers to the deepest problems of philosophy the Church Fathers knew as little as any other human being. Christianity has never represented itself as working on the basis of rationalistic philosophy alone. Its ultimate principles are mysterious declarations which it has received through revelation, while it promises rich rewards of the spirit to those who honestly follow the orthodox chart of life. And legion have been the witnesses to the fulfillment of its promise.

A second problem of almost equal importance survived the Synod of Constantinople for prolonged and violent discussion. The relation of the God-Man to God had been settled in the doctrine of the Trinity, but what of his relation to man? How could the Divine Spirit become human, and what was the relation of the human nature to the divine nature of Jesus Christ? The controversy on this point, if not quite so bloody, was almost as bitter as the Arian dispute. The various theories which were one by one rejected by the Church need not be described. Not until the Council of Chalcedon in 451 did the Church settle upon a formula, again one which simply included all desirable aspects of the problem without much attempt at fusion. By the formula of Chalcedon, Christ is represented as a union of two distinct natures, one divine, the other human, so that he was fully man and fully God at one and the same time. He had not one nature, made up of the union of the two, else neither nature would have been perfect. For if the human nature had been mingled with the divine he would not have been true man, since his human nature would have been superhuman; at the same time he would not have been true God, for his divine nature would have been lowered by being mixed with the human. The two natures, each complete and distinct, were present in him at the same time.

It is only natural that the strength of the Church had been deeply undermined by the centuries of controversy. The formula of Chalcedon, while advocated by the majority of orthodox Christians in the east, and adopted at the direct suggestion of Pope Leo I of Rome, met the dogged resistance of large sections of the Church, and coincided with the growing weakness of the Empire in holding itself together. The chief disagreement was in favor of what was called Monophysitism. The Monophysites, as the term indicates, thought that the two natures had in Jesus been fused into a single divine-human nature and were not kept distinct as in the Chalcedonian formula. They refused to listen to compromise, and continued the controversy until the Church weakened and could not prevent them from seceding in large blocks. The churches which had thus withdrawn themselves became organized as national Christian churches, and continued bitter against the main body, though they differed from it on only this obscure point of doctrine.

Justinian, who, with his immediate successors, was the last Roman Emperor who seemed to be moved by the spirit of ancient Rome, did all in his power to bring the Monophysites into harmony with his orthodox court. But he failed entirely. Particularly did the great body of Egyptian Christians, with their head-quarters in Alexandria, refuse to yield. There is no definite time of their breaking away, but by 550 the separation under the leadership of the Patriarch of Alexandria was an accomplished fact. The Egyptian branch, called the Coptic Church, survived even the Mohammedan invasions, and still exists as a separate body of more than 600,000 members. Similarly in Syria, with headquarters at Antioch and Edessa, the main sentiment became prevailingly Monophysite, and the Syrian Monophysite Church emerged, likewise still surviving, though with only about 80,000 adherents whose head has still the title Patriarch of Antioch. The same thing happened earlier in Armenia, where the Christians rejected the Chalcedonian Creed for Monophysitism in a synod in 491, and have persisted since that time as the Armenian or Gregorian Church, whose followers number much over a million.

The Church that remained, with its center at Con-stantinople, not strangely put its major emphasis there-after upon orthodoxy. When it distinguished itself from other groups of Christians, it was to call itself the Orthodox Church. Settlement of the fundamental problems was followed by an official settlement of de-tails, so that the Church had by the seventh century an approved formula for almost every conceivable phase of its doctrines, upon whose absolute acceptance it insisted with intolerance of any reservation. So while the eastern orthodox Christians expressed themselves, as will be described in the next chapter, in asceticism and mysticism, a rigidity settled upon their ideas which quite put an end to intellectual curiosity or vigor.

CHURCH AND STATE IN THE EAST

Meanwhile, as an organization, the Church in the east had become comple ely a department of the Government and its politics. Following the example and laws of Justinian, the Church, even in smallest matters of ritual and discipline, was subject to imperial direction. Justinian made a most important announcement of the relation between Church and state, important not only for the eastern Empire, but also for the west. He declared: "Among the greatest gifts of God bestowed by the kindness of Heaven are the priesthood and the imperial dignity. Of these the former serves things divine, the latter rules human affairs and cares for them. And, therefore, nothing is so much a care to the emperors as the dignity of the priesthood, so that they may always pray to God for them." The distinguishing part of this statement is the word "therefore," and what follows. Church and state both come from God, says Justinian, and *therefore* the state must supervise and regulate, as he goes on to explain, the Church. This has been the theory of the orthodox Eastern Church in all its relations to government ever since. The Eastern Church has never, like the Roman, tended to take over the functions of the state for itself. It has frequently tried, by ecclesiastical influence in court, to control the policies and activities of the state, but has never revolted and attempted to form a divine state in opposition to the government, nor declared that the government should in theory be subject to the Church. As will later appear, Justinian's statement expresses perhaps the most fundamental difference between the Roman and Eastern Churches.

While the Church in the east had thus been developing into a department of the state, the Church in the west was becoming an institution with quite a different conception of its purpose and proper methods. The distinctive development of the west was the result of the totally different situation in which Christians there found themselves from that which prevailed in Constantinople. After Constantine built Constantinople and established a rival capital in the east, there was still, with very exceptional intervals, an Emperor in the west until 476. But with few exceptions the western Emperors were men of secondary importance as compared with the great Augustus in Constantinople, so that the officers of the state in the west had far less prestige with which to meet the advancing claims of the clergy in their new legal powers. And particularly was Rome almost at once different from Constantinople in that the seat of the western Emperors was more often Milan or later Ravenna than Rome herself, so that while the Bishop or Patriarch of Constantinople was a court functionary, the Bishop of Rome, with his great traditional prestige in the west, was practically free from political supervision. As the Empire grew steadily weaker in the west, therefore, the political independence of the Church and Bishop of Rome inevitably grew to proportions undreamed in the east. This general tendency was strengthened by the fact that to Rome came a succession of relatively strong men, while at the time of crisis the See seemed providentially always to be occupied by a vigorous character.

THE GROWTH OF PAPAL POWER IN POLITICS

When Constantine took over the Church, he had great respect for the Roman bishop as an influence in the Church. As has been stated, when he tried to settle the Donatist quarrel his first recourse was to ask the Bishop of Rome to mediate. At the failure of this attempt, however, Constantine called a council under the presidency of another conspicuous churchman, where proceedings were carried on with the representatives of the Bishop of Rome taking no prominent part. But at the close of the council, when it was desired that the results of the council be proclaimed by the churchman whose position would give it the greatest weight, the Bishop of Rome, or the Pope, as he may be called for convenience, was asked to publish the decisions of the council, "since you held the governorship of the greater diocese." There seems, then, to have been at this time no notion that it was the inherent right of the Pope to sanction all dogma and law of the Church before it could become such. And yet the prestige of his See above any other in the west, his influential position, was obvious to all. So desirable did this preëminence of one bishop over the others seem to Constantine, that he used Rome as a model in his attempt to build up other great centers. Thus in laying the foundation for the legal patriarchal system already discussed, the Council of Nicæa proclaimed that the Bishop of Alexandria should have such authority over all the bishops in Egypt, Libya, and Pentapolis, as had the bishop in Rome over his constituency; and the same authority should be exercised by the bishops at the capitals of the other great divisions of the Empire. That this system of patriarchs was never completely worked out has already been indicated. But the point to be noticed here is that the Bishop of Rome was regarded, in such an ideal system, as of coördinate power and prestige with several great bishops, though the power he had already acquired was made the model for the others.

While the system could never be applied fully in the east because of the terrible doctrinal disputes, the power of the Roman Bishop steadily increased. The Popes, as representatives of the western point of view were consistently in favor of Athanasius and the Nicene Creed. Rome, then, the strongest single bishopric in Christendom, came during the Arian controversy to stand to the orthodox easterners as their court of appeal over against the Arian appeal to Constantius. In 343, the two brother Emperors united in calling a synod at Sardica (modern Sofia), which was patronized predominantly by westerners. Athanasius was upheld, while one canon of the synod (resolutions passed at synods are called "canons") made the whole procedure into general Church law. It declared that when a bishop was deposed anywhere in the Church he might appeal directly, disregarding his metropolitan and patriarch, to Rome. The Pope could then declare a new trial, and his decision on the case would be final. The east had little to do with this canon, and never recognized it, yet its passing was if nothing else an important witness to the reaching of Rome for power over the entire Church, and her support therein by the Christians of the west. Indeed sixty years later this canon of the obscure council of Sardica was blandly declared by Pope Innocent I to have been enacted by the Council of Nicæa, and hence to be universally binding.

A century later there came to the papacy Leo I (440-461), called properly the Great, the most important single champion in advancing the claims of the Papal See. He was elected in the midst of a most distressing period of disorganization. Rome had been successfully invaded by one barbarian nation, and all social stability seemed disappearing. The Empire was represented in the west by a succession of weaklings to whom no one could look for any relief. The great provinces of Gaul, Illyrium, Spain, and Africa felt little or no connection with the imperial puppet at Ravenna. The Roman organization had completely collapsed and each section got along as best it could. But as the prestige of the state diminished, appeal to the civil powers of the clergy naturally became yearly more common, while the ties of the Church seemed the only ones left to hold the old Empire together. This situation acted to strengthen the authority of the Roman prelate. Leo legalized the custom of appealing to Rome, and insisted that his decision was final. Some years before, in the case of a judgment of Innocent I, Augustine had exclaimed: "Roma locuta, causa finita," —"Rome has spoken, the matter is closed." But while it had come to be the opinion of many pious people that Rome's word was thus final, many thought quite the contrary, so that not until Leo did Augustine's statement express an actual law. For in a dispute with an archbishop Leo won a complete victory, and then turned to Valentinian III, the weakling Emperor dallying in Ravenna, and obtained from him a remarkable decree confirming him in his action. In this decree Valentinian stated that Rome was the chief seat of ecclesiastical power in the Empire and an important force in keeping the peace of the Empire. Accordingly the Bishop of Rome's decrees were universally to be respected, and were binding at once upon all men involved, independent of the Emperor's sanction. Valentinian concluded with the astonishing declaration that thenceforth whatever a Pope had ever sanctioned or should ever sanction should be valid law of the Empire.

The tendency is very clear. While the imperial power in the east was becoming more local but continuing to uphold its power of rulership, the eastern Church was steadily becoming more and more a mere department of the state. But in Rome, as the power of the state diminished, the political power of the Church, and of Rome as its center, was rapidly growing, for powers supposedly belonging to the state were becoming more and more the prerogatives of the Church, and preëminently of the Papacy. The Pope was now not only a legal judge, but a law-maker, whose law was binding upon all the Empire.

A few years later the struggle already described over the matter of the relations of the divine and human elements in Christ had dragged itself nearly to the end. A council was held at Ephesus which came to conclusions which Leo did not approve. He denounced the council to no avail as a Council of Robbers, but at the timely death of the Emperor at Constantinople who had called the council and upheld its action, Leo found support in a new Emperor, who called for him the Council of Chalcedon. To Chalcedon Leo sent by his representatives a letter, called usually his "Tome," in which he pointed out the traditional attitude of Rome, and this, with the imperial approval, turned the battle. The theory set forth in Leo's Tome became the doctrine of the Church, and the council at the end sent its actions to Leo for his sanction as head of the chief center of Christianity. But Leo was chagrined, with his victory, to find at the same time a canon which declared the bishops of Rome and Constantinople, co-ordinately, to be the chief heads of the Church. He refused to sanction this canon, but it was none the less regarded as valid in the east.

THE DOCTRINE OF "PAPAL SUPREMACY"

It was Leo who set forth the doctrine of "papal supremacy" in its first definite form. The doctrine, one of the most important ever formulated by man, claims that Peter, the chief of the apostles, was told by Christ that he was the rock upon which Christ was going to build his Church (Mat. 16, 18 f.). Some years later, Peter came to Rome where he founded the Roman Church, and at his death was followed by a successor. Now as all bishops are successors to the powers of the apostles by the doctrine of "apostolic succession" already described, so the Bishop of Rome has ever since, it is claimed, succeeded to the powers of Peter, that is, has ever since been the chief over all other bishops. This doctrine, first formally proclaimed by Leo, was by no means original with him. The Roman Church has claimed ever since the time of Leo that this doctrine had been believed by all true Catholics from the time of Peter himself. Agreement upon this point between Catholics and non-Catholics can never be hoped for. The historical evidence for the tradition is very slight. The statement in Matthew's Gospel is not beyond suspicion, and that it meant originally all that the Church has claimed for it is dubious. The evidence that Peter ever went to Rome is late and inadequate, while there is no evidence at all that the successors of Peter at Rome succeeded to the powers which the Church claims Jesus had committed to Peter. Further, the doctrine won its way to acceptance in the west only against great opposition, and has never been accepted by Catholics in the east at all. Roman Catholics believe the doctrine not because there is adequate historical evidence for it, but because what evidence there is has been authoritatively interpreted by Church tradition. This tradition has always been guided infallibly, it is believed, by the Holy Spirit, and hence can establish for the faithful what is otherwise inadequately attested.

This is the theory which Leo did not originate, but brought forward and proclaimed in order to protest against the imperial declaration that the Patriarch of Constantinople was of equal authority with himself.

The division of opinion on this point marked the beginnings of the final separation of the followers of Rome from those of Constantinople. From the point of view of the Emperor in the east, in order to preserve his imperial dignity, his Patriarch at Constantinople could hardly be allowed to admit inferiority to Rome. At the same time Rome could not admit the claim to equality of Constantinople without giving over her growing ambitions for rulership, political as well as religious, in the west. If there were two heads of Christendom, so far as Rome was concerned there was no head at all, no authority in the Church.

That is, the great question of how the Church was to find its voice as a whole and speak, had had two solutions. The east had accepted the method of councils, whose findings should become state law by decree of the Emperor, so that a rebel against the Church could be treated as a criminal. The west, lacking all imperial machinery by this time worthy of the name, was still to work on the problem for centuries, but was already tending to answer it by pointing to Rome: "Roma locuta, causa soluta." In such a view of the Church, two Romes were impossible, just as any superiority of the Roman Pope was impossible for the eastern solution. Since neither was inclined to yield to the other, they inevitably drifted apart.

The Roman Bishops, indeed, rapidly pushed their claim, so that in 484, as a result of a doctrinal controversy, the Pope formally excommunicated the Patriarchs of Constantinople and Alexandria, and ten years later all who had disapproved of Rome's action were likewise excommunicated. The process of excommunication is, as the name indicates, a refusal to admit a person or persons to share in the sacraments. That is, if Rome excommunicated the Patriarch of Constantinople, it would refuse to allow him to partake of sacraments which faithful followers of Rome had consecrated, while Rome would refuse itself to partake of a sacrament at the hands of a Patriarch. Since the whole being of the Church consisted in these sacraments and the grace of Christ therein transferred, excommunication was the form of banishment from Church membership. When Rome thus cursed the Patriarchs of the east, it severed all connection with them, and refused to recognize their organization as a part of the Christian Church. Pope Gelasius I, who issued this second decree of excommunication, went on to write a letter to the Emperor at Constantinople, in which he declared his complete independence of state control in religious matters. In it he admits that from God there came at the same time two forces into the world, the power of the state and that of the Church, the one ruling the earthly affairs of man, the other guiding his eternal relationships. So far Gelasius is in agreement with the eastern theory as it was soon afterwards expressed by Justinian. But Gelasius goes on to say: "Of these two

powers the importance of the priests is so much the
greater, as even for kings of men they will have to give
account in the divine judgment. Know, indeed, most
clement Son, that although you rule over the human
race, yet as a man of devotion in divine matters you
submit your neck to the prelates, and also from them
you awake to the matters of your salvation. In making
use of the celestial sacraments and in administering
those things, you know that you ought, as is right, to be
subjected to the order of religion rather than preside
over it. Know, likewise, that in regard to these things
you are dependent upon their judgment, and you should
not bend them to your will." Gelasius goes on to say
that as the priests are obedient in civil matters, so the
Emperors should obey in matters of the Church: Rome
later, as will appear, went much further than this in
her claims, but already she had developed a policy
exactly opposite to that of Constantinople. For whereas Justinian was soon to assert that there were two
powers on earth, the state and the Church, and that
therefore the state must guard the Church, Gelasius
said that the Church must look after the state. To be
sure Gelasius' declaration of the independence and
supremacy of the Church as over against the state referred only to religious matters. But it is important to
see that Rome here has begun to regard herself as
above the state; the Church, and especially the Papacy,
is the rule of God to which all men should be subject,
even Kings and Emperors.

In this break with Constantinople Rome was tem-
porarily victorious. But during the sixth century the

Papacy, like all Italy, fell into desperate straits.   It was largely subservient to the eastern Emperor, and had little authority anywhere.   Even the bishops in the west were unruly, while all society was in a state of indescribable deterioration.   At this juncture there came to the papacy Gregory I, called the Great.

THE FINAL INDEPENDENCE OF THE WESTERN CHURCH

Gregory (590-604), as the ideal monk and a writer of popular religious works, had long been the idol of Italian Christians and was finally made Pope against his will in response to an irresistible popular demand. His personal popularity brought all classes to his feet, so that he was able to save the organization and discipline of the Church from the anarchy into which it had rapidly been falling.   The Roman See had become very wealthy in estates left it by the wills of pious Christians all over Italy; indeed the Pope controlled larger resources than any other governmental official in the peninsula.   For the last fifty years these had been most corruptly administered, but Gregory had them tended in the best possible spirit of fairness and the funds publicly distributed.   The Pope had long taken the place of the Emperor as the pensioner and provisioner of a large part of the Romans.   This public service Gregory performed so conscientiously that when one begger died in want who had been overlooked in the distributions the Pope himself did penance for his carelessness.   The care of Gregory for the city at once made him its master. Gregory's power was felt even against the Lombards. It was largely papal money which supported the army of defense at Rome, and when the Lombards attacked the city he broke off in the midst of a sermon to go out and encourage the guardians of her walls. He soon succeeded even in making a treaty with the Lombards for the protection of his people, independent of imperial sanction.

But Gregory was followed by weak Popes, and for another century the fortunes of Italy continued to recede. The Lombards were cutting off the power of the imperial representative in the west whose residence was in Ravenna, called the exarch, so that he became only a figurehead, while the jealousy existing between the Lombards and the Catholics continued bitter. The Lombards were converted to Catholicism from Arianism during the seventh century, but the Popes refused to appeal to them for help in governing Italy. Whether consciously or not, this refusal marks the beginning of the future policy of the Roman See, namely, always, when possible, to get its political support from some non-Italian power. The Popes could not hope to keep or develop a political power of their own in Italy if they were under the patronage of a strong Italian prince, who, in uniting Italy, would leave them only with their spiritual prerogatives.[1] In this case the

---

[1] This direful policy was consistently followed by the Papacy until 1929, when for the first time since the collapse of the Western Empire the Papacy recognized the legitimacy of a non-ecclesiastical rule of Rome. The step can only mean that the Popes have abandoned their old territorial ambitions, and have recognized at last that they must aspire for religious supremacy without any direct political dominance.

Popes chose recognition of the political supremacy in Italy of the exarch of Ravenna, precisely because he had no real power, while they continued opposition to the Lombards. The result was of course the desolation of all Italy.

Rome's weak relation with the imperial power in Constantinople, which consisted in little more than recognizing the right of the exarch to approve or annul a papal election, apparently left the Popes free to gather political power for the Church. But the situation had many disadvantages. The government at Constantinople in the seventh century was turbulent and weak, and yet it used what strength it had in support of the claims of the Patriarch to equality with or superiority over, the Pope. Such a situation could not last long. The inevitable separation of Rome and Constantinople came in connection with a new doctrinal dispute.

There arose in the east a protest against the use of images in worship. Contrary to the early worship of Christians, the Church of the seventh and eighth centuries had come to use very widely pictorial representations of saints, illustrations of the Old Testament or the Gospel, pictures or images of Christ and the Virgin. Since a large part of the population could not read, the use of these representations was defended on the grounds that they were necessary for the instruction of the ignorant in sacred story. A Christian was supposed to revere the picture, but not actually to pray to it, as a modern Catholic is supposed to pray *before* his crucifix but not *to* it. But to some people a sacred image seems to be actually an idol however it might be regarded by the worshipper. A great movement began in the seventh century demanding that all images, paintings, and sacred objects be destroyed, and that the worshipper, facing bare walls, pray without any material object or medium. General practice, however, had so associated sacred illustrations of the faith with prayer, both in private and public worship, that the suggestion of destroying them aroused the fiercest indignation. The controversy is known as the "Iconoclastic [i.e. image breaking] Controversy." Rome expressed the deepest desire of the entire west and of all but a minority in the east, when it took an uncompromising stand in favor of using the images. But the Emperors took the other side, and again the east was torn with riots, persecutions, and torturings in a religious dispute. Rome and the west were little affected, but their sympathies were still further turned away from the power at Constantinople. The exarch, surrounded at Ravenna by Lombards, and soon to be driven by them from Italy, was at last excommunicated by Rome. Shortly afterwards, in 732, the same year as the great battle of Tours, the western Church formally excommunicated and anathematized all Iconoclasts. The Emperor, as an Iconoclast, had of course an Iconoclastic Patriarch, so that the curse of Rome practically applied to all eastern Christians. When the Iconoclasts were later overcome in the east, and images restored to the faithful, Rome and Constantinople resumed ecclesiastical relations, though each was ever ready to denounce the other on the slightest pretext. But Rome never renewed its recognition of subordination to the Emperor in Constantinople. The Popes had finally done with the old Empire.

The Church of the west had thus completed its cycle. Taken up by the Empire as a promising organization to help in cementing and inspiriting the state, it had constantly grown in power while the Empire decayed, until now it could declare its independence of the Emperor without experiencing the slightest shock. But different indeed from the institution which Constantine had adopted was the Church which now again became free. For the Church had taken from the Roman state its ideal of government, and much of its legal system and methods of administration, while the early Christian conception of the unity of the Church had been developed into a growing ambition that the Church, led by the Papacy, some day rule everywhere over all the affairs of men. Yet if it seemed that the Roman spirit of organization had been reincarnated in the Church, so far as externals went it was still in the weakness of infancy. Gelasius had declared the Papacy superior to the state; Augustine, as will be seen in the next chapter, had dreamed of a time when the Church might rule heaven and earth without a secular state at all; but such a time was not yet. Still the Church, if superior to the state, was urgently in need of a political organization to supplement her own futile attempts at rulership.

THE NEW ALLIANCE

Now that the break had at last come with Constantinople, where was to be found the power of God in state
affairs which the Church would recognize as her earthly
complement? The natural choice would seem still to
have been the Lombards, who under Liutprand were
driving the last relics of imperial power from Italy, and
who had achieved the best government of the generation. But again the Pope knew that the Lombards
were too near, and that recognition of Liutprand as
his temporal co-ruler, while it would mean the peace of
Italy, would involve surrender of his own political
liberty.

It was thus a remarkable coincidence that in the very
year when Rome broke from Constantinople the
Franks, by conquering the Saracens at Tours, emerged
as a power conspicuous over all the world. Shrinking
from the Lombards, who must be conquered if they did
not soon subdue the Papacy, the Popes turned to the
new power of the Franks. For in spite of the confusion
of Frankish politics and the chaos of the Church in
Gaul, the government of Charles Martel alone offered
the Papacy any promise of security without immediate
political domination. It marks an epoch in the history
of all Europe when the Pope made the decision, and appealed for help against the Lombards to Charles Martel
in France.

For the Church, under the leadership of Rome, was
the only political institution surviving antiquity which
rose above the jealousies of local tribes into a view of

mankind as a whole; it alone had any formulated tradi-
tions of government, law, and ethics. Weak as it was,
it alone could speak to men with the authority of age.
It still represented itself to the world as the Catholic
Church, although Rome had achieved its unity of doctrine and its political prestige at the cost of losing
practically all the old Catholic Church outside of Italy
and Gaul. Though it still formally communed with
Constantinople, the connection meant little because of
the mutual jealousy of the Pope and the Patriarch;
while the great Churches of Armenia, Syria, Egypt,
North Africa, and Spain had either broken off on a
doctrinal difference, or had been swept away by the
tidal flood of Islam. It had gained its experience in
politics, its taste for universal control, and its vague
but lively temporal ambitions, by inheriting one by one
the functions of the dying Roman officials. But costly
as had been the process which had produced Roman
Catholicism, the institution which at last emerged was
to be the dominant force in Europe for nearly a thousand years. The appeal to the Franks is significant,
then, as it launched the Papacy upon its tremendous
career in European politics.

CHAPTER III

THE BEGINNINGS OF MEDIEVAL CHRISTIANITY IN ROMAN CIVILIZATION

AT the same time that the Roman Empire was giving shape to the great organization of the Church, Roman society was influencing other aspects of Christianity no less profoundly. The Christian Church went on from Roman society into medieval civilization not only as a great force in politics, but also as the guide of all man's thought, action and aspiration. How man should worship, what are the ideals of conduct, and what one should regard as the meaning and purpose of life, these were questions which the Church not only professed to answer, but was everywhere for a thousand years accepted as having finally answered. The peculiar character of medieval civilization was very largely a product of the universal acceptance of the Church's teaching on these points. And yet the teaching neither was what has been explained as primitively Christian, nor was it a medieval product. Rather was it under the influence of the late Roman Empire and its problems that the Church's teaching about worship, ethics, and philosophy took the forms which so long molded the thoughts and standards of human life. This part of the teaching of the Church can accordingly best be understood in the light of the conditions out of which it emerged.

THE CHURCH AND PAGAN SOCIETY

The adoption of the Christian Church by the state raised at once a fascinating problem. Two institutions which had considered themselves fundamentally antipathetic had suddenly been joined together, and were forced to adjust themselves to each other. The great problem was whether the Church should adapt itself to Roman society, or Roman society to the Church. It would be expected that each would have conceded much to the other in disputed points; but actually the concessions seem largely to have been made by the Church. Christian historians, from Eusebius on, have searched the records exhaustively to find evidence of an elevating influence in Roman society as a result of the Churchly ideals, but in general with little success. The social degeneration which was increasing when Christianity was taken over by the Empire continued in general quite uninterrupted by Christian teaching, while it is an open question if on the whole the injury done to the Empire by the fearful disputes in the Church did not far outweigh the benefits conferred by Christian standards of morality.

But if it is difficult to discover traces of beneficent influence of specifically Christian ideas in the history of the late Roman Empire, it is clear that all Christianity was profoundly affected by non-Christian practices and conceptions. For the Church had more to do in adapting itself as the state religion of the Empire than to develop its organization. In Constantine's time it had already become difficult for a non-Christian to get any public employment, and in less than a century it was a public crime not to be a Christian. And yet by nine-tenths of the inhabitants of the Empire in 312 Christianity had not been accepted, while to most of them it was quite distasteful. A simple manner of worship, for example, such as was celebrated in the second century, had no appeal to men immersed in the ideas of polytheism, which meant a god for each phase of life, each to be propitiated at the fitting time. The pagan Romans were quite honest in insisting that a Christian who denied the existence of their gods was an atheist, and an enemy of the state and society, for all his talk of the One God, and of the peculiar divine man Christ. The manner of thinking of the Roman "man of the street" could hardly be changed by the fact that the Emperor wanted to use Christianity as an organization to help unite the Empire. The eventual concession on this matter made by the Roman citizen was formally to renounce his gods, a very great concession, and one which was slow in becoming universal. The concession made by the Church was no less: she adopted, one by one, the essential ideas and rites of paganism as her own.

The concessions made by the Church to the spirit of the times in the period before Constantine have in part been already indicated. In general they were at first toward meeting the more serious pagans halfway in their conception of what a religion should offer. What the more thoughtful pagan wanted of religion was primarily that it form a bridge to unite him with God.

As a part of the material universe, he aspired to rise above it into the pure life of God, to become himself divine. To accomplish this ambition he turned to religions of various kinds, which offered in their secret passwords and rites of initiation a bridge to deification. It has been shown that the Church very early represented herself as a saving institution in this sense, with little reference to the fact that Jesus himself had apparently never dreamed of founding such an organization. But the step once taken, the Church early began to offer the features attractive in other organizations for human salvation. Particularly in the increasing emphasis upon orthodoxy, upon the correct passwords to the future life, and upon the forms of admission to membership did the influence of these religions most appear. For, like the mystery religions, before a candidate for admission into the Church could be received into the brotherhood he must be instructed in the principles of the faith as a catechumen, and then purified by baptism. Only if thus properly prepared, could he witness and share in the great mystery of the Church, the miracle of the Mass, and therein partake directly of the nature of Deity.

For what the heathen mind wanted was that the Deity be made accessible, which meant for almost all that he be made accessible in material form. While some found this in mysterious ceremonies, the less intelligent made use of idols, but still the desire of the age was fundamentally the same. For the gods, with their division of power, seemed to ordinary men much nearer and more real than the one God who was master in all

phases of life. The one God seemed to them vague
and remote while the gods could more easily be thought
of as persons, their likenesses represented in idols,
which could be kept in the house, or set up on the ship,
field, or battle standard which it was desired that the
god protect. Or the presence of divinity could be
guaranteed by wearing an amulet of some kind charged
with divine power. That is, the philosophical man, like
the ordinary man, wanted to be in close communion
with Deity, but the philosophical man wanted by philosophy and ceremony to be elevated to Deity, the ordinary man wanted Deity brought down to him. And
this latter function the gods and their images filled
better than Christianity in its simple original form, so
that the ordinary pagan was quite honest in thinking
that one who went over to Christianity left religion
behind him. Some provision for the honest needs of
such men had to be made if the Church was really to
hold and satisfy them. The Church was thus compelled to offer virtually a polytheistic religion.

THE ASSIMILATION OF PAGANISM INTO THE CHURCH

The process of taking the lower pagan ideas of religion over into Christianity had already begun by
Julian's time, and was making rapid advances. One
way in which paganism had multiplied its gods was in
the reverence and worship paid to departed heroes, and
to the founders of cities. These were regarded as
"animæ sanctiores," were reverenced as patron deities,
and to them altars and temples were built. The Chris-

tians began the assimilation of polytheism when a
similar reverence came to be paid to the martyrs.
Martyrdom was regarded as atoning for whatever sin
had been committed in life, so that the soul of the
martyr went directly to God. But according to pagan
ideas of the time, the soul never got very far away
from the old body, just as superstitious people today
are apt to think that ghosts linger near cemeteries.
So the Christian believed that near the corpse of a
martyr was hovering a soul which was in the immediate
presence of Deity, and had itself completely experienced that greatest desire of the religious soul, been
made like God by having seen Him as He is. After
the persecutions, then, it became the custom to put the
bodies of martyrs into churches, or else chapels were
erected over their graves, or where this had not been
possible the Christians had gone to the martyrs' graves
to pray and offer the Mass, in order to get near to a
spirit which had immediate access to God. Such a
spirit, it was thought, would secure from God what the
pious petitioner desired. The spirits were called upon
as they still are, with the cry "Ora pro nobis," but
soon prayer through the martyrs became actually
prayer to them. They came to be in Christian eyes
the true "animæ sanctiores," or, briefly, "sancti," to
whom man could properly pray for protection and
help, particularly against the dread attacks of demons.

That the attitude was recognized by the Church at
the time as quite parallel to the pagan attitude is made
clear by several contemporary writers. Theodoric
said to the heathen: "The Lord has introduced his dead

into the temples instead of your gods. They are in truth the leaders, champions, and helpers against the demons." Augustine wrote in a letter: "When in the peace which came after the numerous and violent persecutions, crowds of heathen who wished to assume the Christian religion were kept back because, having been accustomed to celebrate the feasts connected with idols in revelry and drunkenness, they could not easily refrain from those pleasures so hurtful and habitual, it seemed good to our ancestors that for a time a concession should be made to this infirmity, that after they had renounced the former festivals they might celebrate other feasts in honor of the holy martyrs, which were observed not with the same profane design, although with similar indulgence." When, after persecutions had ceased, martyrs became rare, the new heroes of the Church, the hermits and extreme ascetics, came to share the same honors.

The process went on beyond this, however, for when a heathen temple was taken over it was frequently dedicated to some saint, who was honored with precisely the same rites and prerogatives as had been given to the old god. So far as popular appeal went, the old god had simply changed his name. The most famous instance of this sort of invasion of paganism into Christianity is the case of the old Roman Pantheon, a temple in Rome dedicated primarily to Jupiter Vindex, but used as a temple for deities of all sorts. In 607 this temple was given to the Bishop of Rome, who purified it and dedicated it to the Virgin and all the Saints, and from this dedication became fixed one of the most important of the church festivals, that of All Saints, which still survives as the popular festival of Hallowe'en among those who little dream they are perpetuating an institution of Roman paganism.   There was no way in which the martyrs or ascetics were officially selected as worthy of honor as saints.   Reverence of any individual martyr began spontaneously and locally.   A community where a martyr was buried revered its own martyr and made offerings in his chapel, but only gradually did any one martyr come to have validity as an intercessor in the minds of all Christians.   With them came also the angels, who may have been worshipped in prayer from early times.   The whole practice of praying through, or to, what were really minor deities was of course much protested against, but went on in spite of all protest, so that by Augustine's time its use was defended, though with warnings against abuses, and with attempts to fit it into the philosophy and theology of the Church.

Above all this saint worship, which also produced a popular Christian mythology to replace that of the gods, emerged the Virgin Mary, who had been regarded with deep respect from the second century, but who in the fifth and sixth centuries was officially accorded unique honors.   A tremendous controversy raged in the fifth century as to whether, since she was the mother of Jesus, and Jesus was God, she might be called the Mother of God.   Some argued that she was not the mother of his divine nature, but only of his human nature, and hence, profoundly as she was to be revered, she was not to be called God's mother.   But this

seemed to many Christians somehow to be reflecting
upon the deity of Jesus, so that, with cruel persecution
of those who disagreed, the party prevailed which
called her the Mother of God. The prayer of Apuleius
had been addressed to the "Queen of Heaven," ascrib-
ing to her the names of Ceres, Venus, Minerva, Diana,
Proserpina, Juno, Bellona, Hecate, and Isis. Christians
likewise prayed to the "Queen of Heaven," calling her
the Virgin Mary; and by weaving about her legends of
miraculous virginity and of translation and coronation
in Heaven by her son, they turned her into a divinity
of more popular appeal than any member of the Trinity, with the dubious exception of Christ.

The revering of the bodies of martyrs and other
saints led to their use as charms in the old pagan magical fashion. Any fragment of the body of a saint, a
finger nail or a wisp of hair, or anything that had been
associated with the saint's body, was regarded as still
haunted by the saint's spirit and hence powerful to
work miracles. People wanted to have the protection
of such a divine object in their houses or on their persons. The greatest teachers from the fourth century
onwards were convinced of the value of these relics.
Chrysostom said that the bodies of saints are the best
possible defense of a city, both against men and demons, more potent than walls, moats, weapons, and
armies. Ambrose cried out in a sermon: "Let others
heap up silver and gold; we gather the nails wherewith
the martyrs were pierced, and their victorious blood,
and the wood of their crosses." Ambrose himself insists that, when he wanted to consecrate the basilica at

Milan, he had a vision which told him to dig in a certain spot. Here he found the bodies of two large men with heads severed, but perfectly preserved, even to the blood which was still fresh in their wounds. He asserted that these were two martyrs whom he called by name, though no one else had ever heard of them, and he carried their bodies in procession to the new altar. Ambrose said, "The age of miracles returned. How many pieces of linen, how many portions of dress, were cast upon the holy relics, and were recovered with the power of healing just from that touch. It is a source of joy to all to touch the extremest portions of the linen that covers them; and whoso touches, is healed." Such accounts could be multiplied. The Church went mad on the subject. Of course there were protests from conservative Christians. Vigilantius asks scornfully, "Why do you adore by kissing a bit of powder wrapped up in a cloth? . . . Under the cloak of religion we see really a heathen ceremony introduced into the churches." He thought that prayer was done by the living, not the dead; which St. Jerome thought he had fitly dismissed by asking, "Shall Vigilantius, the live dog, be better than Paul, the dead lion?" One result of the adoration of relics was, of course, that from early times (Augustine mentions it) traveling clerics sold particles of holy anatomy to the faithful. The practice of relic-selling was subject to gross abuse, for the more incredible a story the salesman had to tell about his wares, the easier a market he found, and of course the articles were rarely genuine. It would have taken close examination indeed to distinguish between the relic, or holy charm, which many Christians began to wear and are still wearing, from the amulet worn by pagan Romans to bring them good luck or ward off misfortune.

Many scholars are convinced that the sacrament of the Eucharist, even as celebrated in the early Church, was a direct borrowing from the mystery religions which also similarly made God accessible in material form. Of course many other scholars do not agree with this, but there can be little doubt that once the rite had begun in the Church, the example of heathen rites profoundly modified the Christian attitude toward it. The modifications were only gradually introduced, and are sweepingly denied by Church tradition which insists that the Mass was regarded by the Apostles in exactly the same way in which it is explained today. But no impartial observer can read the references to the Sacrament in the second century, to say nothing of the first century, and compare them with the references to the Mass in the time of Gregory the Great, without feeling that a great change had taken place during the four centuries that intervened. The greatest change was in the application to the rite of the word "sacrifice." The word was used in the second century in connection with the Eucharist, indeed the Eucharist was then called the only true sacrifice, but the term was used in so vague a way that it is impossible to be sure what was meant by it. But in the time of Gregory the Great, the Christian

sacrifice was very definitely a thing which was offered
to appease an angry God or in gratitude for favors, in
just the way in which the heathen had offered their
sacrifices before a campaign or after a victory. The
matter of just how the consecrated bread and wine
could be called the body and blood of Christ was still
not yet settled, but that they not only could be called
so, but really were so, was the firm conviction of every
Christian. Salvation had come to man by the fact that
Christ had offered up his body to God on the cross.
Now again in the Mass the sacrifice could be repeated,
and those who offered it up did the one thing which
more than anything else would please God and incline
him to their favor. Gregory wrote: "The host [the
consecrated bread] offered with tears and the benignity
of the sacred altar pleads in a peculiar way for absolu-
tion, because he who, arising by his own power, now dies
no more, through it in this mystery suffers again for us.
For as often as we offer to him the host of the passion
so often do we renew his passion to ourselves for abso-
lution." And in another place he asks when this offering is made, "Who of the believing can doubt that the
heavens are opened at the voice of the priest, that the
choirs of angels are present in that mystery of Jesus
Christ, that the lowest things are associated in the
highest?"

So long as the sacrifice of the Mass was limited in
efficacy to the uniting of the souls of men with God, it
remained approximately what it was in the second century. But the little wafer or cup of wine which had
been changed into the true nature of God was regarded

as a means by which the power of God could be applied to other ends. Here was expressed the fundamental desire of all religions but the most philosophic. As the vast majority of men everywhere conceive religion, it is a means of getting divine power in their favor, and the most successful religion is regarded as the one that can be applied to accomplish the greatest number of desires of the worshipper. So, in imitation of the magical rites of the pagan sacrifice, processions were made in which the consecrated elements were carried out to fields to make them fertile, or through cities stricken with plague, or besieged. Masses were said to make God propitious to one about to take a journey or for the sake of those ill or in danger, while Gregory the Great himself recommended the Mass as an effective thing in breaking chains of imprisonment, or in case of shipwreck. When a man was ill or in danger, he would vow fifty Masses if he could escape, and the pleasing prospect supposedly made God change His mind in the man's favor, just as the gods of old were appeased in their wrath if one promised a hecatomb. The Church of the age encouraged such pious action.

As the Mass came more and more to be regarded as a heathen sacrifice, so it increasingly was equipped with external trappings and ceremonials borrowed from pagan ritual. Like the heathen, one must now approach the sacred temple of God only after a purificatory bath. The bath had come to be symbolized in the heathen temples by bowls of water outside, from which the worshipper splashed a few drops upon himself as he entered. When the heathen temples were adapted for

Christian use, the same bowls were retained and the practice continued as it still does. Censers and incense, rather than use which before the Emperor's statue Christians had died by the hundreds, were now carried over directly from heathen rites to add sanctity to the altar and the Mass. Candlesticks were in all the churches, filled with lighted candles as prayer offerings burning on altars or before holy images or pictures, though the Christians had earlier been particularly sarcastic against the use of candles before heathen altars and idols.

SACRED IMAGES

Mention has already been made of the controversy over the introduction of one of the pagan methods of bringing a god near to the worshiper, that of making a picture or statue of the god before which prayers were said. It had been clearly demonstrated by the early Christians that this method as used by the pagans was blasphemy, because prayer should only be made to God, and no worse travesty could be committed than to attempt to represent the formless immaterial God in human material form. But the demand of the time for an object of prayer which men could see, or at least for a visual medium through which they could make the God to whom they were praying seem more real, was irresistible, and the Church surrendered to the extent not only of allowing them to make and pray before images and pictures of Christ, the Virgin, and the Saints, but even of encouraging them to do so. The

custom and its late origin are illustrated in the incident
when Constantia, the newly converted wife of Constantine, asked Eusebius for an image of Christ. Eusebius
could refer her to the Old Testament prohibition
against the making of graven images, and proudly ask
her if she knew of a case where the law was broken by
the presence of an image in a single church. But other
new converts continued to ask for images, and men less
strong than Eusebius yielded.

Another reason for the new-felt need for sacred pictures was to serve in decorating the new churches.
Before the period of Constantine there had been some
church buildings, but the insecure position of Christians
in society had made such efforts comparatively rare and
simple. With the legal toleration of Christianity this
situation was ended so that on all sides Christians
began to build church buildings, and particularly did
the great ecclesiastical capitals put large sums into the
erection of worthy structures. Unlike the pagan temples, which had been small round places for priests,
before which, under the open sky, the sacrifices were
conducted, while the worshipers watched also in the
open, the Christian church was to be a place where
large assemblies could come together to hear preaching
and the reading of Scriptures, and where, excluded
from profane eyes, the great mystery of the Mass could
be celebrated before multitudes. Naturally the model
for such a great assembly hall would be the large assembly halls of the day, the royal halls, or basilicas,
where the imperial trials were held. These consisted
usually of a large rectangular hall, with rows of pillars

which yet left a very wide central portion unbroken, while at the end opposite the entrance was built a semicircular addition covered by a semidome, with its floor raised above the level of the main hall. On this platform the judges sat and the trials were conducted. Such buildings were taken as models for the new Christian churches. The altar, filled with miracle-working relics of some saint, was put where the judges' bench had been, the clergy were given seats about it, while the laity stood below in the great hall, and a porch, or double porch, protected the doorway at the far end from the entrance of the unbaptized during the celebration of the Mass. The period was one in which sculptural and architectural impulses were in their decline, and men were losing power of realistic drawing altogether. But the sunset of classic art lighted the new Christian churches with a blaze of color. Artists of the time detested bare walls, and demanded some motifs in which they could work out their instinct for effective use of strong coloring. When not made of colored marbles, the entire walls from the porches to the great semidome over the altar were accordingly colored with figures and designs, all suggestive of sacred theme or story and all done in the most brilliant red, blue, green, and gold. Surrounded thus by such a harmony of religious suggestion and esthetic delight, the priests conducted the bloodless sacrifice and offering of God for the people, themselves clad in magnificent robes of office, while censers and choirs mingled incense and chorus in rising oblation and petition to the world unseen. The spectacles and offerings of pagans paled before such splendor. The need of the human soul for a sense that it had access to God, and that God would come down to it was here at last satisfied. Even the Vandals, when in sacking Rome they entered the courts of the great Basilica Santa Maria Maggiore (which still stands in its glory), blanched before the evident presence of Deity, and left its treasures untouched.

The early Christians would have been amazed and confused in such a serv:.e, seeing all the things they most protested against in paganism brought over into the service and worship of Christ, but the hold of the Church upon the people thereby was given a power which steadfastly endured even during all the periods of weakness and corruption through which the Church passed in the course of the next thousand years. Polytheism, idols, amulets, sacrifice, and ceremony had been produced in Rome as everywhere else, directly by the need of the souls of ordinary men. So in adjusting herself to the religious life of the Roman citizen, the Church found and met the religious needs of the ordinary man of all generations and places. And in taking such a form of worship over to the barbarians she possessed a powerful appeal, gripped them on their own level, fired their imaginations, and captivated and held their loyalty.

ASCETICISM

Similarly in the matter of the moral teaching of the Church, large adjustment had to be made to the life of men in Roman society. The final solution of the problem of the Church's moral standards took a peculiar form as a result of a persistence in the Church, alongside of the ordinary man, of some who carried on the old spirit and ideas of the Christian life, whose standards were impossible of realization by most men. For the old persecuted Christian community had from the first regarded itself as a group of strangers in a foreign land. They had looked upon the Roman government and society as the kingdom of the demons, against whom, by the help of Christ, they were in revolt, trying to save their own souls from the universal perdition of mankind. The "Kingdom of this World," as a material thing, was utterly despised by those who regarded all material life as sinful and transitory, while they looked beyond the material for true life and happiness. Such an attitude is called "asceticism."

The ascetic, whether Christian or heathen, believes in two great contrasting existences, namely the material world and another world which may be called the world of forms, or the world of concepts, the spiritual world, heaven, or God, or any other of dozens of terms used by different forms of religion. But the ascetic believes not only that there are two such contrasting kinds of life, but that man has in his own nature the representatives of each, which are at war within him for his soul. Thus far, almost all intelligent opinion in the late Empire agreed with the ascetic, but it is for the ascetic definitely to choose the life of the spirit or whatever he might call it, by trampling down the material aspect of his life. And the more rigorous an ascetic, the more violently he abuses the bodily part of his existence in the hopes of destroying it and its desires so that he may live always, now and hereafter, the unpolluted life of the spirit. Whether one agrees or not with such a solution of the eternal problem of the warfare of our reason and our desires, it is clear that it represents an honest attempt to live life at its best and noblest.

Asceticism, more or less extremely carried out, had been the attitude of the earlier Church, but even in the Church before Constantine there had been growing a tendency to distinguish between ordinary Christians and those who took the ascetic ideals more seriously. From the beginning of the third century, or earlier, Christians who regarded all bodily pleasure and comfort, particularly sexual experience, as sinful, came increasingly to adopt the expedient of retiring from ordinary life, in the hope of escaping sin by avoiding external temptation. In the earliest period of the Church the more pious who wished especially to renounce "sins of the flesh" used simply to deny themselves life's experiences, men and women alike, and live together in special houses, where they helped each other to be true to their ideals of continence. In the simple-mindedness of the early Church the same houses were frequently inhabited by both men and women. By the middle of the third century it had become clear that this commingling of rigorists was hardly advisable, but still the notion continued that chastity with renunciation of the world was the highest way of dedicating oneself to God. These people, in distinction from ordinary Christians, had taken the "whole yoke of Christ" and belonged to the class of the "perfect," to whom alone applied counsel of perfection. Several grades or degrees of membership characterized the mystery religions as well as Christianity, but the Christian ascetics took their title from the advice of Christ to the rich young man, "If thou wilt be perfect, go sell all that thou hast and give to the poor," etc. Renunciation of all one's property, sexual abstention, and a complete dedication of oneself exclusively to the work of the Faith thus came to mark a higher order of Christians.

Shortly before the Church came under the protection of the Empire, the Christian world was profoundly moved by rumors of a new form of the renunciation of the flesh practiced by Christians in Egypt. For centuries, extreme ascetics, both men and women, worshipers of Serapis, the popular deity of late Egyptian history, had hid themselves in cells or caves opening only by a crevice for air to the outside world, where they had lived their entire lives in an attempt to cut themselves away from the temptations of the body. In direct imitation of these, Christian ascetics in Egypt began to go out into the desert where they could exist with little or no clothing, and live in caves or tiny huts apart from the world. They even shaved their heads, like the priests and ascetics of Serapis and Isis. This adaptation of the heathen practice spread into other provinces. In Syria, where Astarte had been the favorite goddess, Christians climbed to the top of tall pillars where they spent their entire lives, as had the saints of Astarte before them. In the vicinity of the Euphrates a sect of Christians arose who conquered their desires by dancing and howling like the dervishes of the east. But the developments in other places were distinctly later. The beginnings of Christian hermit life were definitely in Egypt, and under inspiration of old Egyptian practices.

Stories of these Egyptian hermits, who, however mistaken we may now regard them, had at least the courage of their convictions, are fabulous. They lived on the most scanty and incredible foods. Of one pair it is told by an ancient writer: "At the usual hours of meals they each took a sickle and went to the mountains and cut some grass there as though they were flocks in pasture; and this served them for their repast." The writer goes on: "The course common to all, so to speak, consisted in diligent attention to the state of the soul, which, by means of fasting, prayer, and hymns to God, they kept in constant preparation to quit the things of this world. They devoted the greater part of their time to these holy exercises and they wholly despised worldly possessions, temporal affairs, and the ease and adornment of the body. Some of the monks carried their self-denial to an extraordinary height. Battheus, for instance, by excessive abstinence and fasting, had worms crawl from his teeth; Halas, again, had not tasted bread for eighty years; and Heliodorus passed many nights without yielding to sleep and added thereto seven days of fasting." Another contemporary records that "Ammoun never saw himself naked, being accustomed to say that 'it became not a monk to see even his own person exposed.' And when once he wanted to pass a river, but was unwilling to undress, he besought God to enable him to cross without breaking his resolution; and immediately an angel transported him to the other side of the river." Other hermits wore no clothes at all. One individual is recorded as having lived fifty years in the clefts of Mount Sinai, entirely naked, and overgrown with thick hair. He refused to see a single visitor, on the pretext that human visitors interrupted the visits of the angels. St. Jerome used to preach that he who is washed in Christ need never wash again.

Such frightful abuse of one's physical constitution, frequently, if not usually, resulted in insanity. Occasionally there is mention of a hermit who went mad and committed suicide, but a modern reader feels inclined often to put down to this cause the great trial of all these ascetics, the frequent appearance to them of the devil in the form of a beautiful woman. The agonies suffered by these pathetic martyrs to what seemed to them the highest life are by no means belittled by supposing that many of their experiences were the hallucinations of broken intellects. When one reads of the imitators of those Egyptians in the North, how they would break holes in the ice and spend whole nights standing to their necks in the water to rid themselves of these horrifyingly enticing apparitions, one feels that it is not for a less rigorous age to view these heroes of the Church otherwise than with profound respect, at least for their amazing strength of purpose.

The movement thus to renounce the world, beginning with St. Anthony in Egypt in the latter part of the third century, first became widely known in the fourth century and immediately called out a host of followers.

Throughout the fourth century, with its terrible doctrinal disputes, these hermits stood firmly by Athanasius, though for the most part they were illiterate, and
could not have understood the merits of the controversy
if they had tried. In times of danger they would get
together in large armies, wild eyed, almost naked, their
skins tanned like leather, hairy as wolves, and come
and parade the streets with candles. If need were they
fought with carnal weapons, but their very appearance
struck consternation into the hearts of Arians, and ex-
hilarated the orthodox with confidence. Miraculous
legends of all sorts gathered about them. Men and
women in crowds rushed to the desert.

MONASTICISM

Of course no such popularity could characterize the
movement without attracting many impostors. The
faithful frequently took out food to these hermits, so
that the life was not without attractions to loafers and
tramps who wanted to escape the increasing difficulty
of life in the Empire. The rigor of class distinction,
the crushing taxes, and the instability of property
which characterized society from the fourth to the sixth
centuries led to a general pessimism which depressed
citizens of the Empire everywhere, and made the prospect of a life free from care most inviting. By such
people the chastity of the hermits could easily be professed while it was secretly laughed at, and the life
otherwise certainly offered few cares to those who
adopted it. It was also very pleasing to one's vanity

to receive reverence from multitudes of one's fellow citizens. Under such circumstances it is not surprising that it soon became apparent that there must be some standardization and control of the hermit life. Several other reasons impelled toward the same action. The lonely exile which some of the more severe ascetics took upon themselves began to appear quite unnecessary. Such men, it was found, were more apt to go insane than the men who lived in little communities of hermits, where all worldly life was excluded, but where they had each other for company an hour or two at least in the day.

Still more serious was the problem of how these religious offshoots from Christianity could be linked more closely to the main body which was steadily feeling the necessity of including everything within itself. There is really nothing essentially Christian in thus going off by oneself to pray and meditate. People of other religions have done and had done the same often enough. Indeed so far as the sacramental Christianity of the organization was concerned, there was at first a definite antipathy to it on the part of the hermits. To men who lived thus in remote solitude, the sacraments were impossible, and no one who had any sense of their necessity would have gone thus away from them. The hermits really imposed the curse of excommunication upon themselves by thus leaving the Church, and yet, without the sacraments, they were regarded as the model Christians of all the world. At the same time they were often outspoken enough in their denunciation of the powerful and frequently luxurious bishops and rulers of the Church. How could this movement be made to help rather than hinder the growing power of the Church?

Solution came to be found for this as for the ascetic life itself, in the colonizing of hermits. The dates are very obscure; for the entire early period of monasticism is so honeycombed with legends that it is impossible to know always what to believe. But by the middle of the fourth century the popularity of the ruder hermit life was clearly yielding to a life where a number of hermits lived in a community with some beginnings of cohesion under a recognized president, and with regular meetings for divine service under a priest. The earliest set of regulations for such a life which is still extant is that of Pachomius, at whose death in 346 there were ten large communities of monks living according to his Rule. But the Rule of Pachomius was soon much improved by Basil, whose instructions for monastic life are still the standard in all eastern monasteries. Here much was made of community life, on the avowed grounds that God had made man a social animal and that in solitary life not only did one cut himself away from opportunities of serving God in loving-kindness to his fellow men, but that he could not reach his full development when left to his own unassisted resources. Manual labor was recommended, excesses of abstinence from food and sleep forbidden, the value of study suggested, while the whole community was dedicated to ministering to the needs of suffering people in the vicinity. A wise provision, ascribed to Pachomius, was continued, that before full acceptance as a member of the community, a candidate must be on probation for three years. Only at the close of this period might he take his vows. The wisdom of such a provision is obvious. Many a young man or young woman would rush off to such an institution on a wave of enthusiasm, and when he had lived the life a few weeks or months discover that he had made a ghastly mistake. If he had already taken the vows he must then choose between committing the deliberate and damning sin of breaking the vows, or continue to lead a life in which he had no interest. During the probation, also, candidates who came up with unworthy motives could be detected. It was clearly for the benefit of both men and monasteries that candidates be received into such a life only with the greatest caution.

The new monastic life, with its provision for the sacraments, gave opportunity to the Church to get this movement at least partially under its control. By supervising the priests in the monasteries, who as men ordained by the bishops were subject to their discipline, the whole monastery could be to some extent controlled. When a monastery showed signs of insubordination, it could be disciplined by being forbidden the sacraments, and, when a new monastic society was being founded, it had to be approved by a bishop, if it wished to have the sacrament administered to the members. The Council of Chalcedon decreed definitely that no monastery be set up which did not first get the approval of the local bishop: "Whoever violates this our order shall be excommunicated, that the name of God be not blasphemed. The bishop of the city must keep a careful oversight over the cloisters."

A famous visit of Athanasius to Rome had profound influence upon western Christianity, for he was an enthusiastic admirer of the new movement in Egypt, and brought with him as specimens two of the hermits of the desert. The Romans were at first repelled by their dirt and uncouthness, but lighted by the eloquence of Athanasius they soon took fire with the same zeal. But it was the great St. Jerome who more than anyone else made the monastic life popular in the west. His appeals were deeply moving: "Though thy mother with flowing hair and rent garments should show thee the breasts which have nourished thee, though thy father should lie upon the threshold, yet depart thou, treading over thy father, and fly with dry eyes to the standard of the cross. This is the only religion of its kind. In this matter be cruel. . . . The love of God and the fear of hell easily rend the household asunder. The holy Scriptures indeed enjoin obedience to parents, but he who loves them more than Christ loses his soul. O desert, where the flowers of Christ are blooming! O solitude, where the stones for the new Jerusalem are prepared! O retreat, which rejoices in the friendship of God! What doest thou in the world, my brother, with thy soul greater than the world? How long wilt thou remain in the shadow of roofs and the smoky dungeons of cities? Believe me, I see here more of the light."

This eloquence of Jerome appealed especially to women, and to women of the most distinguished old

Roman families, who turned their beautiful villas into convents, while crowds still went to the desert of the east.

As in the east there was soon need of a standard of monastic life. Monasteries were scattered all about; some were strict, some loose, while all were faulty in administration. A really desirable solution of how men or women were to live such a life was not worked out until early in the sixth century when St. Benedict of Nursia founded a monastery at Monte Cassino. The date of this foundation is usually given as 529, though that is only approximate. For the new monastery he drew up a Rule, whose practicality was so obvious that it was almost at once imitated throughout the west. All future monastic rules were but adaptations of this famous Benedictine Rule. In Benedict's Rule chastity, the renunciation of all sexual experience, was taken for granted. Great emphasis was laid upon having the monks obedient to the head of the monastery, the abbot, and upon keeping them stationary, so that when disciplined they would not run away. A candidate for admission, after a year's probation, took three oaths: to renounce his old life, to be fixed in his abode at the monastery, and in all things to obey the abbot. With the abbot thus given complete control over the lives of the monks, their manner of living was then carefully prescribed. Two main interests were chiefly to occupy the minds of the monks, worship of God in prayer and praise, and manual labor. This manual labor was to be carefully regulated according to the strength of the individual, so that the strong

would get plenty of exercise, the weak not be over-
worked. Food was carefully regulated, and too strict
fasting forbidden. Certain hours of every day were
given to reading, at which time "there shall certainly
be appointed one or two elders to go around the monastery at the hours in which the brethren are engaged
in reading to see to it that no troublesome brother is to
be found who is given to idleness and chatting and is
not intent upon his reading, and is not only of no use
to himself but is disturbing to others." That is, the
Roman practical genius had at last produced in the
Rule of Benedict a human document, in which a life,
which originally in the interest of the moral instinct had
violated every other aspect of human nature, now was
brought within the possibilities of most men of serious
purpose.

THE DOUBLE STANDARD

The monastic movement, however, had still to be
reconciled with the life of the rest of the Church. Here
was the Church, on the one hand blessing couples in
marriage, on the other teaching the degrading effect of
marriage and the life lived with worldly cares and interests. She was encouraging men to make money and
give her money, and at the same time teaching men to
despise all money. A compromise between these two
was impossible. The ordinary man could not live without sex and money, while the ascetic could hardly be
discouraged from renouncing them. The Church came
inevitably to take official advantage of the old double

standard of conduct, that for the "perfect," and that for ordinary people. To save the dignity of the Church's relations with ordinary men, these two ways of living were officially contrasted not as the good and the bad, but as the good and the better. So in the matter of marriage, the official stand of the Church is today that marriage is a good and holy thing, yet that anyone who denies that virginity is far better than marriage is accursed.

The immediate effect of this double standard was felt by the clergy. By the ordination of monks there was made one sort of clergymen who were called "regular" clergy because they lived by the "Rule"; while to distinguish them the old parish clergy and bishops were called "secular" clergy, because, by having remained outside the monasteries to serve the laity, they belonged still to this world (*sæculum*). But the secular clergy by the monastic movement were in a fair way to lose their prestige if they too did not take upon themselves the higher standard. For before the great monastic movement had struck the Church, clergymen had frequently lived ascetic lives, but there was no rule to compel them to do so, and while they had not always been married men, the members of the clergy, even including the bishops, were married quite ordinarily. But now if the secular clergy were to retain their hold upon the popular mind, they could hardly afford to appear definitely inferior to the monks. In the east a compromise was effected which still obtains: the lower clergy are allowed to marry once, though they may not remarry if left widowed, while the bishops can only be elected from clergy who are unmarried. But in the west the necessity became everywhere apparent that all the secular clergy upon ordination must renounce private property and all sexual life. They gave up their right to marry very grudgingly. A decree of the Pope in 385 threatened with deposition any cleric who married. This proclamation was the first formal decretal of the papacy on this subject, and reflected the almost unanimous attitıde of the Church. A few bishops refused to renounce their wives, but their voices were drowned in the protests of the entire west, which had fully accepted the idea of the sanctity of virginity, and its necessity for all clergymen. The law was for many centuries laxly enforced and had repeatedly to be renewed.

If the influence of monasticism upon popular life was hardly an unmitigated blessing, still it is difficult to see how the Church could have kept its ascetic moral idea at all, except by appeal to the double standard. Called upon suddenly to function as a religion of the Empire, it had at once to offer the masses something within their grasp. To have expected from the Roman crowd true Christian life in its primitive or more ascetic sense would have been absurd and suicidal. The only way the true Christian ideal of conduct, as it was then conceived, could have been retained in practice was precisely by expecting it only of those who by their choice of the clerical calling were presumably interested in religious life. So what the Empire had done was to take a distinction already made to some extent in early Christianity, and give it a sharpness and universality of application, a professionalism, never intended or known earlier. The Middle Ages fell heir to this double standard of morality, in which the Church tolerated the ordinary manner of men's lives, but always held before them an ideal way of living which involved renunciation of this life and its pleasures. The entire medieval view of morality was thus built upon an idea of the inherent sinfulness of this existence and the immeasurable superiority of renunciation and denial of all material impulses and desires. And in the moral life, as in every aspect of life, the Church as an institution was able to utilize this contrast to increase her hold upon men's loyalty. For if the ordinary man lived by the lower standard, if he married, and fought wars, accumulated money, and enjoyed life's pleasures, even if he went into no excesses in these pleasures, he had chosen the lower road, and could only hope to be saved therefrom by the Church.

In the chaos of early medieval civilization in Europe the monasteries, corrupt as they often were, alone kept alive interest in studies and thought. Indeed men of scholarly instincts had no other place in society than in such refuges, where they were always welcome. Furthermore, in the age of devastation beginning with the fifth century when pillage was followed everywhere with fire, and when ignorance destroyed precious relics of antiquity, the monasteries alone, with their libraries for study by the brothers, provided any safe dwelling for the records of the past. It is often hard to be patient with the old monks, when one reflects how many valuable documents they wantonly destroyed. One of the most valuable manuscripts in the world, a fourth century Bible, was discovered about a century ago by a European visitor in an Eastern monastery who found forty-three of the leaves lying discarded in a waste basket, and hunted for years before he saw the remainder of the priceless sheets loose on an open shelf in one of the cells. The writers and manuscripts of pagan antiquity were treated in general thus with scorn by the Christian monks, while piety destroyed almost every fragment of the great opponents of Christianity. Still, much as was destroyed, classical antiquity, to say nothing of the writings of the earlier church fathers, would probably have become a matter of the merest shreds and patches in our minds today but for the existence of these holy and on the whole inviolate Christian strongholds.

THE CHURCH'S EXPLANATION OF LIFE

The influence of the ideas and life of Rome and Greece have thus been found to have profoundly affected the Christian worship and moral standards. But before the classical spirit decayed it gave direction to another aspect of Christianity which can again be understood only in the light of its origin. For Christianity carried over into the Middle Ages from the Roman world a fully developed explanation of the origin, meaning, and purpose of life both for the individual and for the race. The word theology, which is the term for this teaching of the Church, has fallen into disrepute in these days. And yet for a thousand years, at least, the thought of our ancestors was fundamentally shaped and guided by theological conceptions. The hold upon men which Christianity had as a political organization, as a form of worship, and as a system of morality is quite incomprehensible without an understanding of the Church's account of life which all men accepted without question, and in which all these other aspects of the Church found their place and justification.

This work of formulating the teachings of the Church was done by a series of really great men, the Church "Fathers," who lived from the third to the eighth cen-,turies, some in the Greek-speaking east, some in the Latin west. Their writings came to be regarded in the Middle Ages as carrying almost the same infallible authority as scripture itself, though they by no means always agreed among themselves, so that the great problem of medieval "Scholasticism" was to bring their teachings together into a single systematic scheme. These men, Cyprian, Jerome, Ambrose, Gregory, Leo, Hilary, Augustine, to mention only the greatest of the Latin Fathers, can hardly be differentiated here, except to say that of them all Augustine (d. 430) was easily the most important. But if the details of their teachings cannot be described, it is essential that the Church's account of this world be understood as it was carried over from antiquity to the Middle Ages, at least as it would have been explained to men of average intelligence, before one can hope to understand the civilization that to a large extent grew out of it. At the same time, it is important to see that this account of life, in the form which it took, was molded in the first place to meet the needs of men of antiquity, and thereby their influence is still an active force in society.

The early Christians lacked altogether what an intelligent person of the day would have called a philosophy of life. To supply this need was the task of the Fathers of the Church. The east and west approached the question from different points of view, as they thought in different terms. The great controversies described in the last chapter were essentially eastern. What the easterner wanted to know was how to adjust a theory of God's nature to the Christian worship of Christ. And this sort of problem is still the core of religion and thought to the eastern Church, which views religion from the ascetic point of view, as a rising out of the material and low, up into the immaterial world. The easterner wanted to understand and share now and forever in the higher life, of which he was convinced that this life of body and desires was only a twisted shadow.

The western mind was primarily practical and legal, and saw all life from the point of view of how men might live best together and how justice could be maintained. Such people were willing to let the east do most of their thinking about the nature of God, while they themselves were much more interested in understanding divine justice and what was sin; whence had sin come, and how it was punished; how divine justice might be understood as regarding sin, and just how the death of Christ could save from sin's penalties. Also the Church as an organization interested the western mind, and the questions to be settled in the west were

—what was the Church, who were the members of the Church, did membership in the Church itself mean that a man would be saved, and what part was the Church designed to play in human society.

SIN AND FORGIVENESS

Christian truth, as it appealed to a thoughtful Christian of the west from the fifth century onward, began thus with the problem of sin as a legal problem of guilt. Every man who has ever lived, since he inherited the fallen nature of Adam, was regarded as a sinner, that is, as one who at the trial of God would be pronounced guilty and sentenced to hell. How then are men to be saved? God decreed absolutely an eternal torment in hell fire as the just punishment for those who do not do his will. Now if God relents, and excuses some or all from the punishment, he has plainly changed his mind, altered his attitude, and this it is impossible for God to do, since he, like the Roman conception of pure justice, is blind to personal differences, and unchangingly relentless in making penalties follow crime. If God pardons those who ask him, merely for the asking, his justice is a myth. Or, as it was popularly regarded at the time, there existed a contract between God and the devil, by which all sinful souls belong to the devil. God could not in justice break his solemn contract.

It was to make it possible for God to save man without any alteration in God's justice that Christ became a man and suffered, though explanations of how Christ altered the situation varied widely. But the explanation found in both Augustine and Gregory the Great, and which seems to have represented contemporary opinion best, was in connection with God's contract with the devil. For Christ, a sinless being, took upon himself the sin of the world. The devil did not recognize that Christ had only the sins of others and was not himself guilty, and hence made the great mistake of breaking the contract by taking an innocent man. For Christ died and was taken by the devil to hell and only then did the devil see his mistake. Christ burst out of hell, taking therefrom the just people of past ages, and led them up to heaven. God's obligation to the devil is now at an end. For, as Augustine says, "since the devil had most unjustly slain him who was without any desert of sin he may now justly lose those whom he for desert of sin holds in his power." Or, as Gregory frankly put it, the divinity veiled in humanity in Christ was a bait held out by God to the devil to see if the devil could not be tricked. In addition Christ is regarded as having functioned as a mediator between God and fallen man so that man and God could be reconciled. For God was angry with man for his sin and must inflict punishment. Christ took this wrath and punishment upon himself, so that God can now excuse man from punishment without having decreed punishment in vain. The one thing certain is that in Christ all difficulties disappeared, and that now God may forgive men and restore them to the original condition of the first created man.

Yet forgiveness is not to be distributed carelessly.

Man must meet God half way. A great controversy divided the western Church for years as to just how those who are to be benefited by the death of Christ are selected. Was the death of Christ something which might benefit any man who wanted to claim it, or was the choice of beneficiaries made only by God? The western Church never wanted to make too definite an answer to this question. For if God chose out what individuals were to be benefited, it seemed to take away all incentive for aspiration from men. Why try, if one's own efforts did nothing, and it was entirely for God to say what sinners he would save and what not? On the other hand if man by his efforts or will could claim the benefits of Christ's death, this represented God, the omnipotent, as taking a humiliating attitude, beseeching men to accept his favors. Some people preferred accordingly to say that God did the choosing, rather than that he was vainly beseeching men to do so. The Church came to permit both views, and itself to stand for a compromise, though the compromise was always very vague. Man and God coöperate, somehow, in man's claiming the benefits of Christ.

If the source of the impulse was disputed by which man turned to God for pardon and restoration, the method by which Christ's merit was transferred was clear enough. The sole agent empowered to distribute Christ's grace and saving benefits was the Church. Christ while on earth had founded his Church, subject to Peter as his representative, and with full power to act in his name. In baptism the Church washed away all the guilt of original sin, while in the

Mass it restored strength to the convalescent soul, and in the discipline of penance it looked after and removed sins which were committed after baptism, and which otherwise would have put the soul back into the state into which Adam's sin had plunged the human race.

In the great doctrine of penance the Latin Church expressed itself most idiomatically. The legal instinct of the West could not be satisfied with too light an avoidance of the penalties of sin. That the man who sins and then repents and is forgiven should fare as well as the man who did not sin at all seemed quite wrong. Gradually the conception grew that this difference was made up in punishment either here or hereafter, here by self-imposed suffering or deprivation, or hereafter in the fires of a place called purgatory where a man stayed and suffered a length of time proportional to his sinfulness. It seemed, for example, to Gregory the Great, that he who has done something not allowed must abstain from doing something perfectly allowable which he would like to do in order to make amends for his fault. Fasting and giving alms were the two most usual ways of making amends, or "doing penance." A virtuous act could be applied to one's own account, or to someone's else, even to help a dead friend or relation who might be supposed to be having difficulties in purgatory for his sins. This idea led to great abuse by the Church in her appeals to men to give her their property. But the starting point was in the legal sense of the westerner that sins required punishment. Penance and purgatory, while admitted in the east, have characteristically never received there any such prominence as in the west.

THE CHURCH

As regards the divine foundation, the Church, and its purposes, the west was taught by Augustine that the true Church is the Church Invisible, made up of the souls of those who are finally saved. Together they form the body of Christ. But this Invisible Church is reflected on earth by the Church Militant, the earthly organization. In it are many not members of the Church Invisible, yet the Church Militant is the only approach of men to the Church Invisible. Because of the imperfection of the Church of this world God supplements it by a government of kings and magistrates. "The Holy Church," says Gregory, "because she is not sufficient in her own strength, seeks the assistance of that rhinoceros," that is, the secular rulership. But this is only a temporary solution. The time will come when this temporal rulership will pass and the City of God, Augustine's word for the Church Invisible, will rule all this world and the next, if this world has not been destroyed. For while the Visigoths were attacking Rome, Augustine saw not a cause for pessimism but a beginning of the end of the old world of sin, after whose destruction the new world of God could be established. But Augustine died without seeing this happen, and his prophecy has not yet been fulfilled. Still the Church must adapt itself to the rhinoceros. Meanwhile the Church Militant, the Church of this world, must with God's help continue to fight against the powers of darkness. As she disciplines men with penance, heals them with God's grace in the sacraments, they may find in her solace in this world, and confidence at the great tribunal.

RELIGION AS A LEGAL SYSTEM

That is, the Roman mind took the Christian religion and made of it a great legal system. God is primarily conceived of in terms of the ideal Roman Emperor. He has absolute power, his word is law, and he himself is bound to abide by his decrees; for he cannot make or unmake them at will but must always follow justice, into whatever difficulty it may lead him. Crime and punishment, contracts which when broken by one side relieve the other of obligation, the careful balance of penalty with guilt, these concerns of a legal mind gave shape to the theology of the west as it was commonly taught, and nourished the medieval man in his interest in law and justice. The Church taught all men that before the tribunal of God they were guilty and worthy of damnation but for the mediation of Christ and his Church. Her power over men was, with the appeal of her higher inspiration, frequently also the tyranny of one who threatens to betray the criminal at the bar of justice if his demands are not complied with. The Middle Ages were by this view of life steeped in a sense of guilt and a fear of punishment. Of course the Church offered in her worship, particularly in the charming cult of the Virgin, a beauty to which many today turn with wistful eyes.   But with the beauty went always, at least implicitly, the relentless compulsion of universal law.

So the soul of the dying Roman Empire did not die, but survived as the soul of the Church, still worshipping largely in its old way, still dreaming of universal rulership, still thinking in terms of law and justice and organization, still retaining the double standard of morality which Roman society forced upon it.   Whatever may be one's opinion today, the man of eight centuries ago would have been unhesitating in his judgment that the Church was the noblest Roman of them all.

BIBLIOGRAPHICAL NOTE

THE great library of books written on the subject of these chapters can fortunately be reduced drastically in recommending books for the beginner. Many are out of date, or are apologetic works designed to prove the validity of some denominational theory, or are technical studies for an expert, or are just popular and superficial. With all of these eliminated there is much of value left, but very little in comparison with the original mass. No attempt is made to name more than a few books with which one unfamiliar in the field might well make a beginning.

Of the rapidly increasing number of descriptions of the religious background of Christianity much can be gained from Gilbert Murray's *Five Stages of Greek Religion* (1925), W. Warde Fowler's *The Religious Experience of the Roman People* (1911), T. R. Glover's *The Conflict of Religions in the Early Roman Empire* (1912), S. Angus's *The Mystery Religions and Christianity* (1925), and H. R. Willoughby's *Pagan Regeneration* (1929). Of this list Murray, Fowler and Willoughby are most important, since they are written with a sympathy for the religious values of pagan religions which Angus and Glover lack. Angus has just published a second and much better book, *The Religious Quests of the Græco-Roman World* (1930), in which the religious and philosophical background of Christianity is reviewed exclusive of the mysteries which he had already discussed. Of Church Histories in the field the latest great work is by B. J. Kidd, *A History of the Church to A.D. 461* (1922), in three large volumes; it is interestingly written, and packed with most useful information, though one should be reserved in agreeing too quickly with some of the judgments in which he shows a strong Christian censori-

127

ousness, or apologetic fervor for Anglicanism. The best Church History is by Karl Müller, *Kirchengeschichte* (1919 to date), not yet completed in its revised and enlarged form, and unfortunately still in the German. Müller's writing is as beautiful as his thinking is precise. On the whole the best study in English of the Early Church is Adolf Harnack's *The Mission and Expansion of Christianity in the First Three Centuries* (2nd Engl. Ed. 1908). Harnack is one of the immortals whose work it is hard to think will ever be anything but profoundly useful, though younger members of the "History of Religions School" can not accept his Ritschlianism. So his great *History of Dogma* is regarded by most scholars as less reliable a guide than the *Leitfaden zur Dogmengeschichte* (1906) of Loofs. This latter book was much used by J. F. Bethune-Baker in his *An Introduction to the Early History of Christian Doctrine* (2nd Ed. 1920), which is the best book for a beginner who reads only English. On the persecutions the facts can be gleaned in brief in E. G. Hardy's *Christianity and the Roman Government* (first published 1894), and H. B. Workman's *Persecution in the Early Church* (1906). Dr. Workman has also a work, *The Evolution of the Monastic Ideal from the Earliest Times down to the Coming of the Friars* (1913), which is the best introduction to early monasticism.

Of collections of source material the most important single volume is by Carl Mirbt, *Quellen zur Geschichte des Papstums und des römischen Katholizismus* (4th Ed. 1924), in which an extraordinary body of material for all periods of the Church is presented in the original languages. *The See of Peter* (1927) by Shotwell and Loomis sets forth in translation all the most important documents for the history of the Papacy in the Early Church, and illuminates them with highly valuable notes. In *Fathers of the Church* (1928) F. A. Wright has compiled a very interesting book of selections from the writings of the Latin Fathers. There are two other useful but uninspired collections of material from the sources in the period, B. J. Kidd's *Documents Illustrative of the History of the Church* (1920), two volumes, and J. C. Ayer's *A Source Book of Ancient Church History* (1913), both translating the material into English. The Fathers can be had more *in extenso* in *The Ante-Nicene Fathers* (1867 ff.) where the complete or most important works of the Fathers of the first three centuries are collected and translated. *A Select Library of the Nicene and Post-Nicene Fathers* (1890 ff.) is by no means so complete, but is a large set of books with many of the most important writings of the fourth and fifth centuries.

For scholarly bibliographies the reader is referred to G. Krüger's *Handbuch der Kirchengeschichte* (1923 ff.), which is itself not especially interesting to read, but is one of the most convenient and reliable books of reference. The Catholic view on any point can always be checked in the *Catholic Encyclopedia* (1907 ff.); the best Catholic Church History is in German, by Joseph Kardinal Hergenröther (5th Ed. 1911 ff.).

INDEX